D0447748

A Democratic Constitution for Public Education

A Democratic
Constitution for
Public Education

PAUL T. HILL AND ASHLEY E. JOCHIM

The University of Chicago Press ❋ *Chicago and London*

Paul T. Hill is research professor at the University of Washington Bothell and former director of the Center on Reinventing Public Education. He is the author of many books, most recently *Learning as We Go*, and coauthor of *Strife and Progress*. Ashley E. Jochim is a research analyst at the Center on Reinventing Public Education.

The University of Chicago Press, Chicago 60637
The University of Chicago Press, Ltd., London
© 2015 by The University of Chicago
All rights reserved. Published 2015.
Printed in the United States of America

24 23 22 21 20 19 18 17 16 15   1 2 3 4 5

ISBN-13: 978-0-226-20054-5 (cloth)
ISBN-13: 978-0-226-20068-2 (paper)
ISBN-13: 978-0-226-20071-2 (e-book)
DOI: 10.7208/chicago/9780226200712.001.0001

Library of Congress Cataloging-in-Publication Data

Hill, Paul T. (Paul Thomas), 1943– author.
    A democratic constitution for public education /
Paul T. Hill and Ashley E. Jochim.
        pages cm
    Includes bibliographical references and index.
        ISBN 978-0-226-20054-5 (cloth : alk. paper) —
    ISBN 978-0-226-20068-2 (pbk. : alk. paper) —
    ISBN 978-0-226-20071-2 (e-book) 1. Education and
    state—United States. 2. School management and
    organization—Law and legislation—United States.
    I. Jochim, Ashley E., author. II. Title.
        LC89.H555 2015
        379.73—dc23

                    2014012243

♾ This paper meets the requirements of ANSI/NISO
Z39.48-1992 (Permanence of Paper).

Contents

Preface

This book is the product of twenty years' work on one question: Can a different kind of governance lead to better outcomes in public education? This question stems from the consistent finding that mandates and rules intended to improve schools instead prevent problem solving and adaptation to students' needs and educators' abilities.

We knew about, and felt a degree of sympathy for, proposals to abandon public oversight entirely, in favor of a social market in which government would fund public education but not regulate it. However, we were convinced that as long as K–12 education was publicly funded some form of public oversight was necessary to ensure taxpayers' funds were spent defensibly and children's interests were ultimately served.

In the course of our twenty-year inquiry we investigated a number of ideas. Site-based management of schools within the existing governance framework is one.[1] Another is a more radical transformation of governance based on the idea that public schools could be redefined as schools operating under funding and performance agreements with government agencies.[2] We also closely tracked what happened when localities and states tried to put these and other governance reform ideas into practice.

What became increasingly clear over time is that the pressure for political accommodation, and thus to accumulating regulation, is strong. Local school boards and state governments may promise to give schools a great deal of freedom, but over time they take it away. The takings of freedom are incremental and often based on the worst cases rather than on general problems. But it is striking that they are not based on any proof that a given constraint is good for all schools or makes them more effective. Public governing bodies tighten the screws over time because issues come up that get their attention, and because they can.

This first became evident with site-based management. In the early 1990s, many school districts encouraged schools to use time and money in novel ways to meet the needs of a changing student population. Superintendents encouraged principals and teachers to think big, but no rules were changed. Schools were encouraged to think of new ways to organize teaching, but they were still bound by the collective bargaining agreement. That meant school leaders had little control over who was assigned to teach in the school and the kinds of work they could do. Schools were encouraged to use time and materials differently, but they did not control their budgets or make purchasing decisions. And so on. In any clash between school autonomy and actual practice, school leaders soon learned that for every freedom they were promised, a rule existed that effectively took it away.[3]

Starting in 2003, some mayors and superintendents tried to redefine their local school districts, to give all schools freedom of action, allow people with new ideas to start schools, make all schools performance contingent, and give families real options. (Leading cities include New York, New Orleans, Denver, and Hartford.) Leaders in these cities recognized that without deep and permanent changes to governance, public schools will be hamstrung by factors like

- restrictive district-wide collective bargaining agreements,
- large central office bureaucracies that control as much as half of all the money spent on public education, and
- state regulations on how schools must use time and money.

These local leaders, in part informed by our concept of a portfolio governance strategy,[4] started transforming public education. Their goal was to transform it from a rule-bound bureaucracy into an innovative, problem-solving public enterprise and, in the process, balance the need for government oversight on the one hand and effective public schools on the other.

In 2012 we published a book on what the pioneer portfolio districts had learned, about how to make public education more open, responsive, and, ultimately, effective.[5] Under a portfolio strategy, city leaders empower schools to control their own staffing and budgets. City leaders also invest in new school development and enable parents to choose among different school options, including charters and traditional public schools. Our research for that book made it clear that the portfolio strategy itself is ever evolving and best understood as a process in transition to a very different end state.

Cities now using the portfolio strategy are in a constant process of change, as control of funds is shifted from a central bureaucracy to school leaders and central offices shrink and abandon many control functions. Portfolio cities also experience changes in the size and composition of their education labor forces. As increasing numbers of students are educated by schools not directly run by the school district, the numbers of teachers covered by a single district-wide collective bargaining agreement decrease. As city leaders seek new schooling options for the students most in need, and withdraw support from the least effective schools, the local supply of schools changes constantly. In the long run these processes will play out; what then does the resulting public school system look like and how does it work?

This book intends to show what that end state will be and how the portfolio strategy can lead to it and reveal what problems and dilemmas will emerge along the way.[6] It does not so much supersede our work on the portfolio strategy as acknowledge its limitations and show where it might be leading, and what policy innovators, philanthropists, and innovative educators can do to build on it.

By defining the end state we hope to encourage policy makers and the public by showing that the turbulent processes of change in public education are leading someplace in particular. We also hope to unite people on the left and right, who hold opposing views about the desirability of public governance versus market processes, in the belief that an effective, innovative public education system can be built on a thoughtful mixture of both.

Acknowledgments

The ideas in this book have had a long gestation. Individuals who listened, presented counterarguments, and demanded clearer thinking as long as two decades ago have influenced what we have written. They include Dean Millot, Michael Kirst, James Guthrie, Lawrence Pierce, Jane Hannaway, Susan Bodilly, Bruce Bimber, Linda Darling-Hammond, Anthony Bryk, David Menefee-Libey, Lorraine McDonnell, Patrick Murphy, Howard Fuller, Bruno Manno, Chester Finn, Joel Klein, Michelle Cahill, Paul Pastorek, and Neerav Kingsland. Some might have forgotten, or would prefer to forget, their contributions.

Mentors shaped our progression along the way. Paul Hill is indebted in too many ways to count to his longtime advisor at RAND, the late Thomas Glennan. And it was through her collaborations with Peter May and Bryan Jones that Ashley Jochim learned to persist on even the thorniest of intellectual endeavors, of which this book is certainly one.

Nearer to the present day we are indebted to colleagues at the Center on Reinventing Public Education, whose critiques and suggestions molded this book and inspired new thinking. They include Robin Lake, Christine Campbell, Michael DeArmond, Betheny Gross, Mitchell Price, Larry Miller, Sarah Yatsko, Deb Britt, and Marguerite Roza. We are also indebted to two anonymous reviewers at the University of Chicago Press and to editor Elizabeth Branch Dyson.

The people who helped, warned, vexed, or inspired us as we wrote this book are in no way responsible for what we have, despite them, written.

1

Why Governance?

Why should a sensible person read a book about school governance? Many well-informed citizens frown upon proposals for performance accountability, charter schools, vouchers, and other governance changes, saying that students do not learn from laws and regulations, they learn from teachers. Just give every child a good teacher, and the problems of public schools will go away. They would be right, of course, if only it were possible to give every child a better teacher without changing the rules by which public schools are governed.

The prescription to give every child a good teacher is deceptively simple, akin to the advice offered by a fictional economist about how to slow inflation: Just pay people less and charge less for things in the stores.[1] This is a sensible approach, if only someone had the power to make it happen directly, which no one does. Since the tools available to policy makers affect inflation only indirectly—and their use often has paradoxical effects, like price controls leading to supply reduction followed by even higher prices—the simple prescription does not work.

In much the same way, bypassing governance to focus only on the classroom ignores the complex forces that ultimately determine who teaches whom and what gets taught. Rules about teacher pay scales, certification, class sizes, local district hiring, and labor contract provisions on teacher assignment all affect who decides to teach, what preparation they have, and where they will be assigned to teach. Rules about curriculum, methods, use of time, and achievement testing affect what is taught. Like inflation, teacher quality, assignment, and performance result from a complex set of factors; anyone who wants to change the results must grapple with those factors.[2] Those who claim these are irrelevant to school effectiveness can rightly be accused of saying, "Pay no attention to the man behind the curtain."

If the performance of public schools is inherently wrapped up in the governing arrangements that oversee them, then improvement is only possible via a change in governance. That is the premise of this book. We consider how to design a governance system that protects children from abuse and taxpayers from fraud without putting a stranglehold on the people and institutions that need to make schools work. In the process, we explore the inherent tension between creating a system that satisfies its adult stakeholder groups that demand protection, deference, or special services on the one hand and providing the most effective schools possible on the other.

This tension between politics and performance is not unique to public education. But, unlike other publicly funded enterprises, it has not been explored to the same extent or depth, in part because reformers have been busy trying to take politics out of schools rather than considering how politics—of which governance is a part—can be managed, constrained, and transformed to serve public purposes.

The Inevitability of Governance

In K–12 public education, governance[3] is the set of arrangements by which actors influence the operation of schools, by setting goals, defining desired outcomes, requiring that certain processes be followed, and forbidding (via penalties) certain behaviors.[4] In the process, governance allocates competing values and purposes for public education, privileging some over others. The boundary between governance and provision of a public service like education is never razor sharp. The preferences and capacities of frontline workers like teachers define how services are delivered. But these preferences and capacities are not literally elements of governance unless they become codified in some way, for example, through laws, regulations, or provisions of contract.

Public education, like all publicly funded enterprises, must have governance.[5] Expenditures of public funds always require some accounting and therefore some rules to protect taxpayers' financial interests. But the public interest in education extends beyond concerns about financial fraud or abuse. After all, compulsory school attendance is premised on the idea that not all parents would or could invest enough in their children's education to ensure full preparation for remunerative work and effective citizenship.

There is always the possibility of conflict, among the preferences of policy makers who define the purposes of public education, taxpayers who pay for it, parents who surrender their children to it, and educators who are paid to deliver it.[6] These conflicts are inevitable and can never be fully resolved, but they can be managed in any time period through agreements about rules and processes for making decisions and managing services. These rules, processes, and methods of managing conflict are governance.

In the United States, educational governance consists of rules, goals, administrative processes, and prohibitions established by Congress, state legislatures, the local school board (either alone or via agreements with employee unions), courts, various regulatory agencies, and bureaucracies (e.g., the State Department of Education and local district central offices). These have grown more complex over time, encompassing more staff and a greater share of the resources used to provide public education.[7]

Our Governance Arrangements Are Accidents of History

BILL COSBY. Suppose way back in history if you had a referee before every war, and the guy called the toss. Let's go to the Revolutionary War.

[REFEREE SPEAKING.] British call heads. It's tails. What do you
do, settlers? . . . Settlers say that during the war they will wear any
color clothes that they want to, shoot from behind the rocks and
trees and everywhere. Says your team must wear red and march in
a straight line.[8]

Anyone who compares the freedoms enjoyed by U.S. private
schools—and even by publicly supported schools in the United
Kingdom, New Zealand, and Australia—has to ask whether U.S.
public schools came out on the wrong side of a similar coin flip.
Most other schools in the English-speaking world are less regulated, more adaptable, and more able to sustain themselves as coherent institutions than district-run schools in the United States.

Governance is inevitable, but particular governance arrangements are products of particular times, cultures, issues, and political events. No other country has a system as explicitly organized
around different religions as does the Netherlands, which provides public subsidies to separate Catholic and Protestant school
systems, all parts of a settlement of deep civil strife. No country
standardizes the school day as much as France, whose education
system was created by strong central government ministry.

No country has a more chaotic governance system than ours,
for many reasons. In the early twentieth century, Progressive Era
reformers sought to rationalize and centralize control of the system by empowering professional administration. They hoped
to create more capable schools—better than the fragmented
one-room schoolhouses that dotted the rural landscape and less
political than the patronage-driven system that dominated urban centers. Thus emerged the local education agency (LEA).
The core of an LEA was an elected school board with power
to make most hiring, spending, and curriculum decisions and a
bureaucracy largely staffed by professional educators. The LEA
was insulated from normal local politics by off-cycle nonpartisan
elections, held at times other than elections for national and state
offices, in order to clip politicians' coattails.[9]

The rationalized system of the 1920s gave way to a larger and politically fragmented system in the second half of the twentieth century. Laws to encourage and broaden the scope of collective bargaining among public sector employees, and to lift traditional bans on teacher strikes, greatly strengthened teachers unions.[10] Perhaps ironically, given the ways in which centralized administration had long limited teachers' power and discretion, these efforts politically reinforced the centralized bureaucracy.[11] Unions, unlike teachers, benefited from a system in which they negotiated with a centralized agency, and the history of unionization in the United States made teachers unions more like their industrial cousins than like the professional associations that dominated fields like medicine and law.[12]

Social activists of the 1960s critiqued the centrally administered school system as unresponsive and unrepresentative of minorities, women, and the disabled and other special groups.[13] Such pressures led to federal requirements for parent advisory councils, new protections for disabled children, and interventions by the federal Office for Civil Rights.[14] Local school boards also created neighborhood councils, assistant superintendents, and special offices within the district, which acted as symbols of concern and were expected to navigate the sea of community complaints.

State education agencies, long disadvantaged by states' commitment to local control, entered the political fray to manage court orders to desegregate the schools. The 1980s and 1990s saw these agencies, as well as their overseers in state legislatures and governors' offices, become more aggressive in their efforts to target financial and academic mismanagement. Court cases that drove states to assume increasing shares of education spending encouraged state legislators to start controlling how the new money was spent.[15] One consequence of this was greater prescriptiveness—in terms of staffing, instructional models, curriculum, and so on. Another was new forms of state intervention including charter schools, district and school takeovers, mayors acting as state agents to run schools,[16] and, most recently, state-run districts.[17]

In this system, private groups that want to influence schools, including neighborhood associations, parents of gifted and special education students, civil rights organizations, business associations, and professional societies, can forum shop. They can try to get what they want (e.g., new programs for language-minority students) mandated by any level of government including the local school board or by the courts; they can also seek funding via a new federal or state appropriation or via an unfunded mandate, which requires schools to do something new without any extra money. As Terry Moe has shown, temporary majorities control future actions by encoding them in rules and bureaucratic structures.[18]

At the turn of the twenty-first century, as many large urban districts headed into academic and financial bankruptcy, the legitimacy of the board, union, and central office combination was seriously eroded.[19] Reflecting the dissatisfaction with the status quo, the use of general government institutions like mayors is on the rise.[20]

The Potential Harms of Governance

Governance of public education is inevitable, but it can produce results that no one wants. For example, our existing governance system creates many barriers to the desired result of providing effective instruction for every child:[21]

State laws about teacher certification and licensing exclude many people who know important subjects and want to teach. In particular, scientists and mathematicians who did not take education school courses are excluded from teaching, while education school graduates, who often do not know those subjects well, are employed to teach them.[22]

Children who are supposed to benefit from extra funding provided by federal programs still have less spent on them than others in the same districts owing to carefully placed loopholes in federal law.[23]

Principals who want to buy better books or online instruction for students in their schools, or to extend the school day by hiring more teachers and fewer administrators, cannot do so because most resource decisions are made centrally.

Schools forced to deal with funding declines can be forced to let go of their best teachers, if more senior teachers elsewhere want their jobs.[24]

Schools serving disproportionate numbers of low-income children in most big cities get less experienced teachers than other schools. This is caused by teacher collective bargaining agreements approved by local school boards.[25]

These, and literally hundreds of other artifacts of governance, can weaken public education and deprive students of learning opportunities.

The Problems with Governance: Civic Mobilization and Unbounded Institutions

Governance matters. The problem with our current governance system stems in part from the failure to mobilize concerned interests on behalf of effective schools. As Clarence Stone and his colleagues have argued, education suffers from a lack of "civic capacity"[26] because concerned interests are mobilized only episodically and even then, around different agendas.

But mass mobilization, even when achieved, is problematic in the absence of institutions that can realistically process competing demands, make trade-offs, and take coherent action. As the Consortium on Chicago School Research learned about the 1989 reforms that made every school accountable to elected neighborhood representatives, some schools improved but a nearly equal number became even more divided and less effective.[27] Adults will mobilize, vote, attend meetings, and serve on committees "for the children," but when faced with concrete decisions, adults can learn that people think differently and value different things about schools. Mobilization does not sweep away politics or remove the need for governance to resolve competing claims and visions about schools.

Our current governance system suffers not simply from a mobilization problem but from an institutional one: Governance institutions meet demands, even competing ones, whenever possible, resulting in proliferation of new rules, mandates, and restrictions. Policies can oppose one another or make multiple claims on the same resources. The political logic has reinforced the institutional one.

Even proposals based on claimed links to school effectiveness—for example, that particular class sizes, teacher licensing schemes, seat time requirements, or administrative structures would lead to increased student learning—are processed as advocacy demands. Such policies are adopted one by one, even in the absence of evidence that they would work equally well in all schools or would be more effective than other possible actions costing the same amount.[28] As described by Dominic Brewer and Joanna Smith, serial satisfaction of demands has led to a "crazy quilt" of policies and constraints.[29]

Some governance constraints arise from perennial problems, for example, schools' tendency to underserve children with disabilities and to try to hand-pick the easiest to educate so they can look good. Rules to protect students against discrimination are unavoidable governance constraints for public schools stemming from a constitutional framework that guarantees equal protection under the law and equal opportunity to benefit from public services.

However, many of the conflicts that led to governance constraints are transitory, stemming from a temporary failure to achieve an objective.[30] Issues arise and are resolved, but their resolutions are encoded in law, policy, or contract. The lack of a professionalized teaching force at the turn of the twentieth century, for example, led to initiatives to license teachers. These types of constraints stay in place even when the problems are no longer present (the norm of college degrees for teachers is now thoroughly established), the problem's characteristics have changed (the types of teachers we need are different), or the parties to conflicts that gave rise to them are no longer active. Teachers and principals consistently say that the rules, as well as the time used to respond to shifting state and district mandates, comply with demands for reports, and attend mandatory meetings, prevent them from doing their best for children.[31] Although in theory the different institutions and levels of government that collectively govern education have their own spheres of action, the boundaries among them are unclear.[32] Any institution of government can impose a requirement, and it does not have to seek the concurrence of any other. Whether these arrangements are well intentioned or not, their multiplication undermines the efforts of those who work in public education.

This Book

How do we design public oversight that does not drive out school problem solving, adaptation to natural variations in students' needs and interests, and the freedom to innovate? This book starts from the assumption that governance can be constrained so as to check the political impulses that undermine the public purposes of K–12 education.

How to fix public education governance in the United States is not a new question. Analysts have suggested many alternative forms of governance, each intended to shift the locus of decision making from local school boards and state legislatures to other entities. Milton Friedman ushered in an era of governance reform thinking. He argued for putting parents in charge. John Chubb and Terry Moe suggested a more complex system, with parents in charge but also some roles for regulators, from whom school operators would need to get licenses.[33] Others have suggested leaving a government-operated school system intact but putting different people—mayors,[34] appointed boards, or state officials[35]—in charge.[36] Still others have proposed creating new institutions to counterbalance old ones—for example, widespread adoption of Louisiana's statewide "recovery school district" that can seize control of consistently low-performing schools from school districts.

These proposals have been tried in limited ways, and some

have made a difference on the margin. However, each contains the seeds of its own limitations—excesses of unregulated voucher schools leading to some students being left behind, mayoral takeover regimes weakened by mayors' political problems or term limits, and state legislators' growing resistance to an aggressive state-run district. Some of these ideas are important, but all of them address only one small piece of the governance puzzle when what is needed is a much broader approach, as we will show.

Why add further to this literature? There are two reasons: first, the politics are changing[37] so that proposals that generated lethal opposition in the past might get a more serious look today. Increasing numbers of large-city school systems are experimenting with new school creation, use of charters and contracts, and experimentation with sources of teachers and new recruitment and rewards systems for educators. Teachers unions, once able to block such initiatives, are still powerful but beset with criticism from former allies and their own members.

The second reason is that the ideas to be presented here are new, more explicit and actionable, and importantly, more complete than any suggested before. This book proposes far more than a tweak of the current governance structure or a change in who is in charge. It proposes a new "constitutional" vision of governance that fundamentally alters the missions of local school boards and the powers they can exercise. It also shows how a rethinking of governance can lead to a more flexible, adaptive, and performance-driven educational system.

The book lays out this vision in detail: how it would work for children, families, teachers, and school leaders and members of governing bodies like school boards and state departments of education. And it discusses the tensions inherent in any governance reform—the political winners and losers and the sustainability of the reform measures over time.

Chapter 2 outlines our criteria for a governance system for public education that serves its public purposes:

- efficient (both effective and productive)
- equitable

- transparent
- accountable
- democratic

Chapter 3 then develops the idea of constitutionally limited local governance of K–12 public education. It describes an alternative to the current school board, which whether elected or appointed has virtually unlimited powers over hiring, spending, and regulation of schools. It describes an entity whose primary mission would be ensuring that every child in the city has at least one and preferably many high-quality schooling options. It also shows how that new entity, called the civic education council (CEC), can achieve its mission more effectively without the power to hire teachers or constrain school autonomy.

Chapter 4 describes the checks and balances that would constrain CECs and other government agencies. These include the local district bureaucracy, state education agency, federal government, teachers unions, and other private agencies that now cogovern public education. It also explains how constitutional governance would empower parents, school leaders, individual teachers, and voters who are not parents. This chapter ends with a review of how a constitutional governance scheme would meet the governance objectives established in Chapter 2.

Chapter 5 shows how this system would create the freedom of action that school and district leaders require to more effectively serve students, innovate and adapt, and constantly search for the best possible options for children.

Chapter 6 focuses on district central office bureaucracy—considering how it would be reduced, how its powers would be checked, and what roles it would still play.

Chapter 7 shows how the new governance system would affect how schools are funded and how funds are used. Students would carry "backpacks" of funding, combining money provided by state, local, and federal sources, which schools could use flexibly, adapting their instructional methods and uses of student and teacher time and technology to the needs of the particular students they serve.

Chapter 8 shows how the system could be enacted and sustained against political opposition and changes in political agendas.

Finally, chapter 9 focuses on the problems of change: how can a system built around a very different governance structure respond to a new set of institutional roles and constraints? How, in particular, can public education in big cities, where the harms of the current governance system are most acute, adapt to the freedoms and incentives created by the new constitutional governance system?

2

What Governance Must Accomplish and Avoid

Governance failures are hardly unique to American education. They are endemic to contemporary political life. But what does it mean to say a governance system has failed to accomplish its public purpose? The study of public policy has long struggled with this question.[1] Should governance maximize efficiency? Or should it promote greater equity? Is transparency more important than effectiveness? These questions are important, and we do not seek to resolve them for governance in general in this chapter. Let it suffice to note that (1) any governance system must achieve many things and satisfy many stakeholders and (2) there will likely be trade-offs between competing values along the way.

In this chapter, we argue that a governance system for K–12 public education must meet five criteria. It must be efficient, equitable, transparent, accountable, and democratic in the American context. We explain these criteria and show how the current K–12 governance system falls short of meeting them all.

Efficient

Governance must be preoccupied with enabling schools to be efficient, both in the British usage of the term, as a synonym for effective, and in the American usage, meaning producing a high degree of output per unit of input.[2]

It is not hard to argue that public schools should be effective in teaching children. Unless they meet that criterion there is no strong justification for taxing citizens to pay for them or compelling children to attend them. In our politically governed schools, however, it is not always easy either to agree on what it means for a school to be effective or to focus policy making on those objectives.

Most people would agree that schools must educate children enough so they can exercise the rights of citizens as well as participate in the modern economy. There is, however, real disagreement about which subjects public schools should prioritize, for example, whether schools that teach children about arts can be considered successful even if their children do not master reading and basic mathematics. There is also some controversy over whether schools' noninstructional functions, for example, maintaining students' family language, maintaining neighborhood identities, and delivering social services, are sufficient evidence of effectiveness in some circumstances. And, of course, there is the question of "effective for whom?" Schools can be effective on all subjects for most children and leave some behind.

Questions about the meaning of effectiveness have been at the center of national education politics for at least thirty years. The standards movement, which spread to most states in the early 1990s, was the first attempt to focus our national debate on what every child should know and do. This movement blended into the current effort to build sets of Common Core standards. Both movements have faced problems of content hierarchy (i.e., are there some gateway skills that should have first priority) and parsimony (i.e., is there a difference between subjects that everyone must master and those that, in a good society, at least some people must excel at?).

We do not profess to solve the problems of content standards. Reasonable people can and do disagree about the exact metrics by which public schools should be assessed. But, schools must be assessed in some way. After all, parents in most states are compelled by law to send their children to school. Parents, and the taxpayers who pay for schooling, must have some assurance that children are learning what they need to know to be self-determining adults. There will always be debate about school performance standards. Moreover, in a period of rapid economic and technological change, standards should be reassessed frequently for their accuracy and completeness. One does not have to think that current standards and tests are perfect in order to hold that schools must be governed in ways that allow them to benefit children and require them to strive for improvement.

Evolving standards and the need for continual problem solving at the school level are not compatible with universal prescriptions about school structure or instructional methods. Requirements that schools adopt particular methods or spend all their money in compliance with mandates emerge in response to political pressures, either by the well organized, as in the case with collective bargaining, or by the popular, as through the initiative process. As long as they serve political ends, they can persist in spite of evidence that they are less effective or more expensive than possible alternatives.[3]

To be efficient then requires a problem-solving orientation in which improved performance is sought, not assumed, and in which leaders are enabled to move resources toward better performing options. Although total flexibility is not possible— students must be protected from discrimination, taxpayers require assurances that dollars are used for their intended purpose, and professionals need reasonable job security—the governance of public education must not impede the search for new approaches that can produce better performance.

Equitable

Since 1964, American public education has been required, both by law and public expectation, to avoid assigning poor and minority students to inferior schools, to avoid admissions discrimination based on race, and to close gaps on achievement and opportunity. Later laws also established the rights of children with disabilities to appropriate services and when possible full inclusion in mainstream classes. Governance must seek equitable distributions of opportunity and outcomes, and these aspirations must be hardwired into it.[4]

In practice, however, our governance system is not built around these aspirations. Despite wide agreement on the importance of equity, our education system tolerates huge gaps in achievement and opportunity. Consider the following:

- Only 57.8 percent of Latino students, 53.4 percent of African American students, and 49.3 percent of American Indian and Alaska Native students entering ninth grade earn a high school diploma four years later.[5]
- Students of color are much more likely to attend schools with inadequate resources and high concentrations of poverty than white students. Additionally, in schools where at least 75 percent of the students are from low-income households, there are three times as many out-of-field teachers teaching English and science as there are in wealthier schools.[6]
- Nearly half of low-income and minority children are unlikely to perform at grade level, graduate from high school, and be ready for college at age eighteen.[7]
- In many cities the same schools have produced the lowest rates of school completion for decades.[8]
- On the 2013 National Assessment of Educational Progress, also known as the nation's report card, just 22 percent of Hispanic eighth graders, and 17 percent of African American eighth graders scored at or above proficient in reading, compared with 46 percent of white and 52 percent of Asian and Pacific Islander American eighth graders.[9]

Core aspects of the current K–12 governance system, including collective bargaining–based placement and retention privileges for senior teachers[10] and unaccountable control of money by central office bureaucracies,[11] sustain an unequal system of schooling. School quality, teacher experience, and central office services and dollars are all unevenly distributed within school districts, and schools in the poorest neighborhoods consistently get the least of everything.[12] These are not inevitable features of schools but consequences of our current governance system.

Good governance entails more than making declaratory commitments to equity; it involves keeping them. That means, at a minimum, that government entities overseeing education must have the resources, freedom, and imperative to seek the best possible options for children.

Transparent

A governance system must be transparent, so that taxpayers, parents, and educators all know how decisions are made, funds spent, and resources used. It would be impossible for educators to meet the efficiency criterion unless they knew how much money they were spending when they decided to buy equipment, hire people, and use employees' time in particular ways. School district and state leaders could not do much to encourage effective use of resources if the costs and dispositions of resources were not visible to them. Although democracy is not premised on full and free access to government budgets, that knowledge could dispel the ever-present suspicion that public agencies are producing very little for the money they get.[13]

Transparency is not a feature of our current governance system, nor is it a criterion that schools and systems even pretend to meet. To the contrary, costs and uses of funds are hidden and often characterized deceptively. Thus, districts hide inequities in per-pupil spending driven by senior teachers' placement privileges by accounting for salaries as if all teachers cost the same.[14] States do not require districts to account for expenditures on a student or pupil basis; instead, they ask for spending reports on broad functions like instruction and student services, which can hide inequities.

A governance system that met the transparency criterion would lead to challenges to previously hidden decisions about what to subsidize and at whose expense. This could cause some upset about how unfunded state, federal, and court mandates are met. Transparency might deter, or moderate, mandates that are now imposed without any clarity about who will get less if some group gets more. Transparency will also make it easier to determine whether one group of students really costs more to educate than another and by how much.

Accountable

A governance system must be designed so that people and institutions are accountable for the results they produce. A governance system that seeks efficiency, equity, and transparency must be able to attach consequences to those outcomes. It cannot be good enough just to try to educate children; if a given institution or approach does not work, the governance system must require a search for alternatives and abandonment of less effective and equitable arrangements for more effective and equitable ones. From this perspective, accountability is focused on doing the best possible for children; consequences for adults (both positive and negative) are by-products of this search.

Under traditional public school governance, accountability has been a grab bag of techniques to motivate employees by praising, shaming, or threatening them. If those techniques did not achieve the desired effect, little more could be done. The existence of schools, teacher placements, and all employees' job security were protected and extremely hard to change, regardless of whether they were working well.

The new accountability contemplated by this criterion, as spelled out in table 2.1, is focused on continuous improvement. Opportunities, rewards, and losses thereof are means, not the

TABLE 2.1 The new accountability: Based in continuous improvement

	Old	New
Goal	Express concern	Get higher performance
Role of measurement	Shine spotlight	Identify cases requiring closer examination
What brings change?	Exhortation, assistance	Intervention: assistance, new options
Consequences for employees	None other than to pride	Chances to perform better; replacement
Options available to leadership	Exhort, provide help; repeat	Assist, switch providers, develop new providers
Who is responsible for results?	Everyone = no one	The person in charge of the institution: the superintendent for the district and the principal for the school. People subordinate to the responsible person experience logical consequences, as employees of an organization that succeeds or fails.

goal. They originate from a desire to improve performance via learning about what does and does not work. School leaders, teachers, and other employees are considered professionals who must work as effectively as they can, make detectable contributions, and do better than obvious alternatives.

Under the new accountability, teachers work in particular schools and experience consequences of school success or failure. As is the case with professionals in the regular economy (e.g., physicians and lawyers), teachers will have strong incentives to make their schools successful but also to maintain their own personal reputations in case they must move on. School leaders will have strong incentives to find and keep the best people and to use pay and work environment as inducements.

Democratic

A governance system must be legitimate and subject to democratic control. This is surely not a universal criterion. In other countries, citizens might regard education as an elite function and not expect any say in its oversight. Yet in American public life, elections uniquely confer legitimacy. This does not mean that Americans expect to vote on every issue or want elected representatives only to take actions that are immediately popular.

As we will see in later chapters, there is considerable latitude in the design of representative institutions and in what powers elected representatives can wield. Some institutions, like courts or regulatory commissions, are insulated from short-term politics but still dependent on elections. For example, presidents appoint members of the Supreme Court or the Nuclear Regulatory Commission. Presidents' political views and accountability to voters affect the decisions they make. These remain democratic institutions despite the time lags and other arrangements that buffer them from the changing politics of the moment.

There is also tolerance for suspension of some powers of elected representatives in emergencies, for example, after Hurricane Katrina. But the inexorable pressure toward elected representation now evident in the demands to restore local control of New Orleans' schools indicates that stable governance solutions must ultimately include democratic elections.

Currently, public education is exposed to political activity of all kinds, from school board elections to constituent casework done by state legislators to parent protests and union-led demonstrations. Educators are supposed to respond to these actions, accepting them as the price of democracy. That is one of the reasons today's public education system has difficulty meeting the first criterion of good governance, efficiency.

A public education system cannot serve children well if competing adult interests and arguments over funds and instructional methods constantly intrude on schools' operation. Although schools need the ultimate sanction of approval by voters, constant oversight and political buffeting is counterproductive.

Is there a way schools can both enjoy democratic legitimacy and be free enough of politics to be effective? Future chapters will suggest that the answer is yes, if voter influence is focused on elections and access to other channels of retail politics is strictly rationed. Schools cannot be effective if "democracy" constrains schools by forcing them to find jobs for powerful people or to divert school funds into contracts with outside groups that need to be mollified.

The idea of insulating K–12 education from politics offends those who favor grassroots control of schools. They often critique mayoral and state takeovers for locating decisions too far away from neighborhoods and parents. Some also object to family choice, saying that although it gives parents influence, it substitutes consumerism for citizenship.[15]

Proponents of grassroots control of schools point to excellent public schools in the United States and abroad that are run by teacher and parent cooperatives. However, they overlook the fact that when these schools fail they can be closed or taken over by government authorities. In these cases, elected officials' authority, and responsibility to ensure children's welfare, prevails over grassroots democracy.

Grassroots control is an option that some schools can pursue conditionally, but a different form of democratic control can supersede it. A good governance system might let some grassroots groups run their own schools, as long as they work for children; it certainly would not require grassroots control of all schools or exempt schools that pursued it from other forms of oversight.

Implications for K–12 Governance

Table 2.2 pulls the argument together. Just as governance can impede progress towards these values, it can also facilitate their pursuit. If we want an effective and efficient K–12 system, then we need to make that system systematic enough to evaluate existing commitments and flexible enough so it can abandon practices that do not work or do not work as well as the alternative. If we want an equitable system, then we must strive for a level playing field at the outset and focus oversight on improving outcomes for the children who have the fewest opportunities. If we want

TABLE 2.2 The criteria and what they mean for K–12 public education

Criteria for governance	Conditions that enable their pursuit
Efficient	An efficient system must be flexible enough to seek out improved performance and be willing to abandon existing ways of doing business when they are ineffective or counterproductive.
Equitable	An equitable system must strive for true parity in inputs and oversight that continually searches for better options for the children who have the fewest educational opportunities.
Transparent	Transparency must be grounded in clear fiscal policies that enable precise accounting for the use of funds.
Accountable	Parties responsible for assembling resources to serve children efficiently, equitably, and in a transparent fashion must be held to account for the results they achieve. If accountability is to be an instrument of improvement, it must be more than recognition.
Democratic	Ultimately responsive to voters via some form of approval, although not necessarily managed in detail via interest bargaining and casework.

a transparent system, then we must design fiscal policies that actually enable an accounting of public funds. If we want an accountable system, then we must be willing to design oversight structures that do not just seek evidence but act on it appropriately. Finally, if we want a system that is democratic, then we must enable voters to check the functioning of that system at regular intervals.

We are not the first to argue that these values are important. But we are the first to trace them to their logical conclusion: achieving these values is only possible via a reconfiguration of the institutions that oversee K–12 education.

Conclusion

These five criteria are not all perfectly aligned. Some are complementary, for example, efficiency, transparency, and accountability. Some are in tension with one another. The most efficient education system is not necessarily the most equitable, transparent, or responsive to political control. It is impossible to eliminate these tensions entirely via clever governance system design; thus a governance system must be able to manage, not hide, conflicts.

The U.S. Constitution does not resolve tensions once and for all. Instead, it deliberately puts different goals and interests in tension and challenges government to find ways to balance and accommodate them all. The governance system we propose for public education follows that tradition by limiting the powers of local elected officials and setting up a system of checks and balances among local, state, and national levels of government.

3

Constitutional Governance

This chapter presents the book's core idea: for the governance system to meet the criteria outlined in chapter 2, its powers need to be constrained and its actions channeled. It is not enough simply to take power over schools away from one entity (e.g., school boards) and transfer it to another (e.g., the mayor). Instead, governance must be limited so that it puts school effectiveness first.

Good K–12 governance will be rooted in a "constitutional" system[1]—one that is not unlike the system of checks and balances that govern broader American lawmaking. As we show in this chapter and the next, this system will result in performance-driven oversight of public education by elected officials, great freedom of action for school leaders, wide open opportunities for people with new and possibly better ideas about how to educate children, and good options for all families.

We call this a "constitutional" system because it is hardwired to focus on effective schools and designed to ensure that government overseers cannot succumb to the temptation to arbitrarily create new regulations, new programs, and so on, whether such actions are intended to secure the allegiance of new groups or existing special interests. While America's current K–12 governance allows for unchecked regulatory expansion, a constitutional governance system would allow public authorities to do only what they have been explicitly empowered to do.

Foundations of Constitutional Governance

K–12 education is a state function, and state law establishes the institutions that oversee and provide it. Of all the institutions that govern public education, the most important is the local school board. In most states, one local board is responsible to provide schools for all children of school age—except those who attend licensed private schools—in a defined geographic area. Although these can be arbitrary, most states set intuitively meaningful boundaries, defining a city, county, or set of neighborhoods that share a tax base and other social and economic identities. Local governance can take account of special local conditions, including population changes, the labor market for teachers, transportation, and the location of buildings suitable for school use.

Some scholars have proposed eliminating local governance of public education entirely and governing all schools statewide.[2] This proposal could eliminate disparities in funding that are now based on differences in local tax bases and effort. It could also weaken local political coalitions that bias decision making in undesirable ways, for example, in favor of political machines, unions, or antispending taxpayer groups. Statewide governance could also eliminate local district borders that allow higher income or white families to create segregated enclaves simply by moving across a district line. In some localities, current school district boundaries are arbitrary, cutting up otherwise well-integrated cities or counties. States could amend this, creating one or a small number of governance units in a metropolitan area.

However, total elimination of local governance is unworkable. Enrollment, growth and decline of neighborhoods, facilities availability, transportation, and availability of talented people are all local conditions that require local knowledge to address. Key decisions about what schools to abandon because they do not work or because parents or teachers want to avoid them must take account of local conditions. None of these issues could be managed well from the state capitol; states that nominally governed K–12 education from the state capitol would be forced to create some forms of local administration in any case.[3]

A new governance system must include a core local unit of organization. However, a constitutional system of governance would define the powers and responsibilities of a local governing body much more sharply than is the case now. In particular, it would set limits on what local governance could do and, by implication, what freedoms school operators would exercise. A local unit of governance could, as we will show, decide whether a given school was performing well enough to justify allowing children to enroll there.

Local governance would not have the one power that has led, under our existing governance system, to the most onerous burdens on schools, that is, hiring and setting terms of employment for teachers and school administrators.[4] Schools would employ teachers and principals and would compete for the best people by offering fair compensation and good working conditions. Schools could not be forced to take teachers cast off by other schools, and teachers that were not employable would not be paid.[5] Local boards could not agree to teacher contracts that could not be funded out of current revenues. Local politicians could not work with local governing board members to get particular people hired, promoted, or fired.

Redefining the powers of a local governing body would not, however, prevent the erosion of school autonomy and adaptive problem solving once and for all. After all, our current system did not originate overnight. It was built incrementally over many years and in response to many different political pressures (some more well intentioned than others). State governments, including legislatures and state administrative agencies continually imposed new rules—for example, about whom schools may hire, how they use time and money, and what instructional methods they must use. A new governance system could become encrusted with new requirements just as our current system has.

TABLE 3.1 Overview of a constitutional governance system

Governing entity	Entity's core powers	What entity cannot do
Civic education council	Appoint superintendent (CEO) and oversee central office actions to open/close schools on the basis of performance agreements	Employ teachers or principals directly Own facilities Restrict the use of public funds, other than to prevent fraud and abuse
CEO and central office	Administer oversight system of public schools	Enter contracts with third parties that impinge on school autonomy
State board of education and state education agencies	Maintain educational standards and decertify school boards or school providers that do not meet those standards	Attach strings to state dollars that restrict how resources might be used to serve students
Federal government	Withhold funds from states or localities that consistently fail to create new options for children in ineffective schools.	Require that federal funds be used differently than state and local funds

The constitutional system limits the powers of local governing bodies so they cannot continually impose new mandates and rules that limit schools' freedom of action. But it does not stop there. It also establishes new roles and responsibilities for other actors, which balance and check the powers of local governance. Table 3.1 provides an overview of roles, checks, and balances. It identifies the key government actors in a constitutional system and sketches their powers and legal limitations. As the remainder of this chapter will demonstrate, the limits on government actors' powers (table 3.1, third column) are more revolutionary than the positive grants of power described in the second column.

This chapter focuses on how local governance would work under a constitutional system. It starts with the core local unit of governance, which we call the civic education council (CEC). It defines the roles, powers, and limitations of CECs. Later sections explain how schools would receive public funds, enroll students and encourage parents to choose, and be held accountable for performance.

Chapter 4 shows how the state board and department of education, the federal government and other institutions including

BOX 3.1 Constitutional powers and limitations of CECs

The state law establishing civic education councils (CECs) would both define those agencies' powers and set limits on what they could do. Under state law CECs would be required to

hire a local CEO on a fixed-term basis,
contract for or charter independent entities to operate schools,
set common performance measures for schools,
approve criteria for determining whether a school can continue receiving public funds,
approve an annual slate of schools to be opened or closed, and
set weights for pupil-based funding.

The law would allow CECs to

issue requests for proposals for a school of a given type in a particular location,
encourage the formation of school cooperatives,
establish a fund to incubate new schools,
make the locality attractive to good teachers by arranging favorable benefit plans for participating schools,
work with local teacher and principal training programs to support unmet needs,

courts and unions, would function, and how a constitutional governance system would limit their actions. Chapter 5 defines a bill of rights for schools.

The CEC

The constitutional governance system rids educational governance of the local school board and puts in its place the CEC. The change is both symbolic and substantive. It is symbolic because it sustains the commitment to local community oversight of K–12 education and substantive because it carefully constrains the power and authorities of local governance.

Consistent with the aim of a more efficient and equitable

set aside limited funds to support central office functions,

review the progress of schools that met some but not all criteria for closure, and

in some states, set local tax levy rates.

The law would forbid CECs to

employ teachers and principals;

set teacher, principal, or CEO certification requirements beyond those in state law;

enter collective bargaining agreements;

employ anyone on a tenured basis;

remove the CEO except for cause;

allocate funds to schools on anything other than a weighted per-pupil basis;

require schools to purchase services from the central office when such services are available from other sources;

own school buildings;

mandate that all schools use a particular schedule, curriculum, or instructional method; and

establish preferential contracts that exempt certain schools from performance measurement or guarantee their continuation regardless of results.

education system, the CEC's powers would be limited to sponsoring the best possible set of schools to serve the students in its geographic boundaries. A CEC would have the power to set common performance measures and criteria for all schools and decide what to do about schools where children were consistently not learning. Councils would have the authority to charter new schools to replace failed schools and to meet otherwise unmet needs. If entities other than CECs are empowered to charter schools, CECs could choose to take account of the schools they authorize, so that if a neighborhood is being well served by others, the council need not insert a new school.

CECs would enter into funding and performance agreements with all sorts of legal entities, including nonprofit organizations, teacher cooperatives, larger organizations that operated schools as one of many missions, colleges and universities, and sole proprietorships. In many cities, groups of schools are likely to aggregate into networks or purchase services from charter management organizations (CMOs). The latter provide both instructionally related and back-office services to multiple charter schools.

The CECs could choose to encourage the formation of cooperative arrangements or multiple-school management groups, but they could not enter contracts with such entities. Their only binding agreements would be with individual schools, whose continuation would depend on their own performance and the availability (or absence) of alternatives for the students they serve. If one organization operated many schools, the CEC would need to enter into a separate agreement for each school. Individual schools, which would receive public funds in proportion to their enrollment, could make their own agreements with networks, management organizations, or other vendors of services, so long as such arrangements complied with laws against fraud and abuse.

The CEC could choose to support local teacher and principal labor markets by negotiating favorable benefit plans with insurers on behalf of schools, although it would not be able to mandate participation. To improve local talent pipelines, CECs could form relationships with local teacher and principal preparation programs. For the same reason, it could also establish a fund to incubate new schools.

Some local CECs might also have local taxing authority, which they could retain along with the authority to set the funding weights attached to students with different characteristics, for example, poverty and disability status. The vast preponderance of public money would follow students to schools, as if students came with backpacks full of cash.[6] Although the local CEC would be able to set aside a portion of funding for data analysis, experimentation, and oversight, the vast majority of funds would arrive at school sites in real dollar terms and be used at the discretion of school leaders. Chapter 7 discusses school funding in detail.

One key limitation on CEC authority is that it must base funding on student, not school characteristics. Students with the same characteristics (e.g., poverty status, English language proficiency, or disabling condition) must bring the same amounts of money to the schools they attend.

The CEC would not have the power to decide to give a particular school more money because of its instructional strategy or cost structure. Such policies are what drive resource inequities in the current system.[7] Schools would receive defined amounts of money, and it would be up to them to manage their staffing and other costs to live within their budgets. Of course, philanthropic organizations and state agencies could decide to pay one-time costs for special equipment or staff training connected with a particular school model, but CECs could not commit to providing extra operating subsidies.

The CEC would not be empowered to mandate general solutions on essentially technical and professional matters for which no one approach is likely to be good in every case. It would be left to individual schools to match instructional and staffing methods to the needs of particular groups of students. Similarly, schools, not the CEC, would judge teacher performance and decide how to make trade-offs, for example, among class size, breadth of curriculum, and length of the school day. CECs would not have the power to find jobs for individuals in the school system or control who teaches in or leads a particular school. Since it would not employ teachers, the local CEC could not enter collective bargaining agreements, although as discussed in chapter 4, unions could organize individual schools and possibly CMOs. Schools could opt into cooperative arrangements to manage the administration of benefit programs.

Because of limitations on their ability to issue new rules or mandates that were responsive to the concerns of individual students, parents, or teachers, council capacity for "casework" interventions would be limited. They could, however, exercise informal leverage by calling attention to issues that might lead to low performance and thus to school closing.

COUNCIL MEMBERSHIP

Who will serve on the CEC, and will the membership be stable enough for members to follow consistent lines of action? Today, school boards in large cities are decidedly political entities, with contested campaigns and strong interest group participation, factors that shape both the types of candidates that self-select into board membership as well as the incentives affecting board members.[8]

Under a constitutional governance system, CECs will have much less complex agendas than today's school boards, which must pass detailed central office budgets, approve principal and central office appointments, deal with collective bargaining, and approve contracts with dozens of vendors. The constitutional system takes most of those activities off their plate. Moreover, school and CMO leaders, not CEC members, will be responsible for dealing with problems that arise in particular schools.

These more focused responsibilities mean that CECs will be less attractive to individuals interested in advancing a particular neighborhood's educational opportunities over another. It will not be attractive to those who would like to institute uniform instructional approaches or school models district-wide. Likewise, those representing the interests of teachers and their unions will have little reason to join the CEC, since schools, not the CEC, will employ teachers.

Membership will become attractive to people who want to engage in analysis of neighborhood needs and support a strategy of differentiation. It may attract those interested in civic renewal. This does not rule out educators or people with commitments to the education of a particular group of students. However, even for those people, their main role will be that of stewardship for all students, not advancement of a particular interest.

MODE OF SELECTION

Many people who wish for more adaptive, less restrictive governance for public schools favor abandoning popular election of school boards in favor of appointment, by mayors, commissions, or other higher level entities. As we have argued elsewhere, a change in mode of selection is always a good idea when a governing body is overly politicized or deadlocked.[9] Any way of selecting board members is open to abuse, and when things are not working out well an alternative can be good, even if it too is imperfect.

Appointment can be a way to break deadlock in existing elected boards, but it too ultimately needs the sanction of voter approval. When state legislatures or courts call for mayoral appointment of a school board, they frequently set time limits or require periodic referenda on maintaining the appointed regime. In Cleveland, where mayoral appointment of school board members has been in place longer than in many other major cities, it was originally imposed by the state legislature but later ratified by citizen vote.

Appointed boards can run into the same problems as elected ones, particularly if provider groups or political machines control appointments. Appointed boards often confound the expectations of mayors and others who appoint them (see Mayor Jerry Brown's experience on Oakland), just as elected boards can disappoint voters. Appointive arrangements can be more stable than elective ones, except when the appointing official is weakened by controversy or driven from office. Then local education governance can be disrupted, even if education had nothing to do with the leader's downfall.

Elections have one overwhelming advantage in the United States: they confer legitimacy. This does not mean that Americans expect to vote on every issue or want elected representatives only to take actions that are immediately popular. But Americans want to think their representatives owe them their jobs and must always ask whether they are retaining citizens' confidence.

In sum, neither mode of selection is always best, or always stable. But other things equal, elected boards are more legitimate. If elected CECs can be kept within their constitutional powers and execute them competently, election is better. However, an appointed board that does its job and does not exceed its powers will have more legitimacy than a negligent or self-aggrandizing elected board. States and communities will need to decide for themselves which arrangement is likely to be the most stable and accepted.

CEC RELATIONSHIP TO SUPERINTENDENT (CEO) AND THE CENTRAL OFFICE

State law would establish that the superintendent or chief executive officer (CEO) would be appointed by the CEC but retain significant independence, with a long tenure and significant autonomy. The superintendent's primary responsibility would be leadership and administration of the school oversight system, including efforts to sustain, expand, transform, close, and/or replace schools.

The CEO would propose and publish, subject to CEC approval, criteria for closure or replacement of school providers by the fall of the preceding school year. Criteria would consider student achievement gains and other measures of student outcomes (e.g., normal progress toward graduation, graduation rates, graduates' ability to pass key courses at the next level of education) as well as school climate and enrollment.

The CEO would also manage an annual parent information and student enrollment process by which all overenrolled schools run their lotteries. Schools might, based on their charter or terms of reference set by either the CEC or CEO, provide admission weights for children living in particular neighborhoods.

The CEO could form or work with an independent organization to manage a risk pool from which all schools can draw funds for special education. At the CEO's discretion, this risk pool can charge different per-pupil amounts to schools based on past rates of expenditures for special education.

A small, nimble central office that complements the constitutionally defined role of a CEC has important jobs to do, including

- assisting the CEO in making judgments about whether troubled schools should be closed by providing data and analysis;
- identifying areas of the city and groups of children that need new options;
- developing talent pipelines;
- communicating action criteria, evidence, and options to parents and neighbors; and
- working with enrollment and transportation managers to make sure kids who need options can get them.

These tasks would require central office employees for coordination and oversight, but many traditional central office functions would be eliminated or contracted out to specialty firms, which would need to compete periodically on the basis of performance and cost. Chapter 5 addresses the role of local bureaucracy in detail.

School district central offices have traditionally been in charge of school capacity building. The district's chief academic officer typically controls the money and sets priorities for professional development programs for teachers and principals, organizing workshops about how to implement new policies, selecting district-wide curricula and textbooks and training teachers in their use, and contracting with turnaround specialists to help troubled schools. Although schools often have small budgets to hire a consultant for a day or two, most of the money for assistance to schools is held in and spent by the central office.

There is a growing literature about how central offices can perform these functions better, without giving up their control of budgets and program choices.[10] However, the constitutional governance system outlined here requires that school districts surrender control of dollars and decision making to individual schools. The money now controlled by the central office would, under state law, be added to the enrollment-based funding schools receive. The money would come without any requirement that it be spent in a particular way. Schools could then decide to use that money for teacher training, for purchase of new materials and advice, or for anything else that improves results. A school with a serious problem in one area (e.g., mathematics) might concentrate all of its spending on advice and teacher training in that area. The same school might emphasize some other subject later. Or, in a given year, it might decide to spend less on advice and teacher training than on a longer school day, new courses, smaller classes in some subjects, or online resources.

Schools could also purchase assistance or materials from any source. Some existing central office units might survive and prosper selling services to schools at their real cost. Schools might avoid dealing with other central office units, preferring to do without the kinds of services they provide or to buy them from other vendors. As in New Orleans, where schools have had this freedom for some time, a new infrastructure of support providers, some led by former central office staff and others by nonprofit entrepreneurs, is likely to emerge.

Development of a new infrastructure to sell schools the kinds of support they need is one of the most challenging but most promising elements of the governance change we propose. There will be fits and starts and continuous improvement in the marketplace. At the moment, CMOs have an advantage because they have had philanthropic support to become integrated service providers like districts. However, as CMOs grow they might encounter problems of over-standardization and lack of responsiveness to schools that could cause schools to seek help elsewhere.

CEC RELATIONSHIP TO SCHOOL OPERATORS

The CEC would contract with school providers to run schools. In some cases, one provider may operate multiple schools, not unlike what CMOs do in many cities. But regardless of how a given provider structures its relationship with different schools, the contractual obligations are between a school site and the CEC. If a CMO-managed school failed, its contract for that school would be revoked, although the CMO could continue to operate its other schools so long as they met performance targets.

OWNERSHIP AND CONTROL OF SCHOOL FACILITIES

In order to ensure a financially level playing field, all schools would pay for facilities in the same way. If the locality had a surplus of facilities, all schools could use them rent-free. But if some schools had to pay rent, all would. In the latter, more likely situation, facilities money would be bundled into the per-pupil amounts that schools receive. Schools would then pay rent from their normal revenue.

It is hard to imagine how owning school buildings would not place the CEC in conflict of interest in some way—favoring some providers with much better buildings than others, or favoring schools that would use CEC-owned facilities over hybrid or online schools that would use little or no space. To prevent this, and focus the CEC's work, ownership of school buildings could be transferred to a different entity. One possible owner would be the city. Another could be an independent real estate trust empowered to own, develop, sell, subdivide, and lease out buildings. Schools could rent space from this entity or on the open market. For more on the idea of a schools real estate trust, see papers by Michael DeArmond and Nelson Smith.[11]

WHAT A CEC WOULD DO EVERY YEAR

The CEC's primary functions are to hire and fire the superintendent, to provide student-based funding for schools, and to decide what slate of schools it will allow to operate in a particular year.

The CEC could hire any person it chose to be CEO. Because the role of the CEO would not be to operate schools but to advise the CEC on the mix of schools needed in the community, there would be no reason to require traditional superintendent certification. A CEC might choose a lifelong educator, but it might also want a person with expertise in assessment, portfolio management, demography, business, or some other discipline.

The new governance system would make the hiring of a CEO a high-stakes decision. Because CECs could effectively regulate schools by forcing the hand of the CEO via threats of firing, CEOs would serve fixed terms. These terms would be longer than the term of any CEC member, so that sudden changes in CEC membership or sentiments could not immediately destabilize the district. State law would enable the CEC to fire a CEO for cause. The CEC could also petition the governor or state superintendent for a waiver to fire a superintendent with years remaining in her term. This would force the CEC to make a strong case against a superintendent and would deter firings over personality conflicts.

The CEC's limited responsibilities would enable it to focus on its most essential function—deciding whether to add to, subtract from, or change the mix of schools operating under its authority. In performing this role, the CEC would work closely with the CEO.

As the state law would require, each school year, the CEO would propose a line of action toward every school. She could propose to sustain, expand, remission, close, and/or replace the school. To set up these recommendations, the CEO must publicly announce criteria for closure or replacement of school providers by the fall of the preceding school year. The CEO would propose an annual slate of actions based on these criteria as well as a consideration of the existing mix of schools and how well particular neighborhoods and student populations were being served, and the CEC could approve all or part of the slate. However, it would not have the power to propose actions other than those formulated by the CEO.

In a normal school year, the CEC would approve the CEO's criteria in the early fall, receive data on the performance of all schools in midfall, receive the CEO's proposed slate of actions in early winter, and approve a final slate of actions toward schools in late winter. It could request additional information on individual schools at any time. Nothing in state law would preclude a CEC from requesting presentations about particular schools. CECs might spend most of their time hearing such presentations and interviewing school leaders.

At its discretion, a CEC might also request information on the overall health of K–12 education in the locality—rates of student growth relative to similar localities, overall improvements in student graduation and persistence in school, and health of the overall labor force (e.g., the numbers of teacher applicants per vacancy, net gains or losses of staff to other localities). These data could help the CEC to put the CEO's proposed actions into context and to encourage more aggressive action when results are not positive.

The CEC could also choose to meet with representatives of groups and neighborhoods who think the options available do not meet their children's needs. The CEC could request that the CEO develop a new option (e.g., a new school or a new initiative within some existing schools) to meet the unmet needs. But the CEC could not order all schools to adopt a particular program or instructional method. The CEC could also meet with school heads and seek advice from any source it chose. It would not, however, resolve complaints lodged against school heads or teachers, lest these actions create ambiguity about who employs and evaluates educators. Schools must remain wholly responsible for employment and assessment of principals and teachers. As discussed below, state law could establish a local ombudsman with the power to refer unresolved issues to the courts or state civil rights or labor boards.

Inevitable Questions and Answers about Local Governance

This section tries to anticipate the most pressing questions that perceptive readers are likely to raise.

WHAT IS THE THEORY OF ACTION BEHIND THIS PROPOSAL?

These changes in governance should lead to improved schools, but not by directly changing what is taught, by whom, or how, but by creating incentives for continuous improvement at all levels. A CEC whose only job is to focus on school performance will be much more aggressive about seeking alternatives and abandoning failures than one that runs some schools directly and is thus reluctant to admit their inadequacies. Likewise, if the CEC does not directly employ teachers or principals or own buildings, it will have greater freedom of action to close or replace low-performing schools and to sponsor experiments with new approaches to instruction, staffing, use of time, and student motivation problems. Autonomous schools will be free to be as effective as their staff and leaders can make them but know that closure is possible if they do not increase student learning or attract parents.

Anthony Bryk and colleagues, building on extensive research about the challenges of providing effective schools in complex urban settings, call for similar system designs, ones that seek to "localize authority, create conditions more responsive to diversity, and provide resources and incentives for local school community improvement."[12]

The theory of action behind constitutional governance does not say that all schools will be effective all the time. It assumes some will not work out and that localities can often find better options if they are open to them. Constitutional governance both empowers and requires CECs to pay close attention to the performance of all the schools they oversee, to abandon schools where children are not learning, and to seek better options when and where they ever become available.[13]

IS THE CEC "DEMOCRATIC"?

Critics might charge that constitutional governance deprives voters of decisions they are entitled to make. Some believe that K–12 education should be a "deliberative space" for citizens and that civic community will shrivel if all important education issues are not negotiated locally, openly, and in detail. People who hold this view consider measures that set boundaries on such deliberation to be antidemocratic.[14]

There is no question that constitutional boundaries on CECs' actions restrict what they can do and thus limits the range of issues that local activists can press them to resolve. Even if they listen to citizens and make school leaders aware of issues that need to be managed at the school level, CEC members will not have the power to dictate a solution.

The question remains: is it undemocratic to constrain CEC powers? There are many forms of democracy, including some under which every issue is settled by citizen vote and others under which officials have great freedom of action, subject only to periodic approval by voters. These different forms of democracy are matched to different situations: issues that need sustained technical efforts or extremely fast response can be democratically controlled, but with time lags and periods of relatively autonomous executive actions. The voters ultimately control even the Supreme Court and the Federal Reserve, but because of the complexity and sensitivity of the issues these institutions handle, they are carefully insulated from short-term political crises, while also facing in the long term important limits on their authority to act. These arrangements strengthen democratic governance by allowing problems to be solved in ways that day-to-day political control would prevent.

There is no reason a priori to say that one ultimately voter-controlled governance scheme is more democratic than another, even if one confers greater discretion on the officials and provides less opportunity for day-to-day citizen input. True, an arrangement that voters cannot touch (e.g., in the 1950s and 1960s the entrenched power of southern Congressional committee chairmen, whose tenure was based on one-party elections from which African Americans were excluded) is undemocratic. So might be an independent regulatory commission that is totally captured by the industry it nominally supervises. However, public enterprises where it matters a lot who is elected (e.g., the military, whose deployment the president can control in detail) are not beyond the influence of voters.

On the other hand, systems that appear responsive in detail, like traditional local school boards or district central offices, can be dominated by small intensely committed groups. Often, access to and influence over such systems are determined by the intensity of group interests, not by representation of all affected parties. As Terry Moe demonstrates, teacher unions often have considerable sway in local board elections by virtue of the fact that they are better organized than the myriad of other "potential" interests that may exist in a community.[15]

Ted Kolderie and others have argued that public education cannot serve children well if competing adult interests and arguments over funds and instructional methods constantly intrude on schools' operation.[16] They argue that, although experts need the ultimate sanction of approval by elected officials, constant oversight and political buffeting are counterproductive. People in charge of getting results should be left alone for periods of time and have no need to satisfy interest groups in the short run; politics should affect their actions only gradually, and with time lags.

By this argument, public education could be treated more like the judicial system or securities regulators. They operate without detailed political oversight, but they remain democratic institutions because elections and deep shifts in public sentiment ultimately affect them.

States, and possibly localities, might choose different approaches to maintaining voter influence and the legitimacy that comes with it. Any approach they choose must, however, retain the clear lines and limitations of local CEC authority as established here. Any ambiguity about limitations could allow local CEC missions to creep in the direction of employing teachers, running schools, and exercising influence on behalf of favored constituents. Under those circumstances governance could gravitate back toward the current system, under which accountability and responsibility, and the rules affecting schools, are ever shifting.

WHAT IF THE CEC IMPOSES NEW RULES THAT ERODE SCHOOL AUTONOMY?

A CEC could try to regulate schools by adding requirements to charters, memoranda of understanding, or contracts established with schools. The first arrangements could respect the limits of CEC authority, but subsequent agreements could be slowly loaded down with new provisions about anything from methods, hours of operation, and payment for services, to teacher employment and pay.

The school bill of rights in chapter 5 addresses some of these possibilities. Schools would have strong warrants in express legal language to resist such encroachments. However, some schools "on the bubble" for closure might accept new de facto regulations as the second-worst alternative.

As chapter 5 makes clear, there is no substitute for alert use of the law by school operators. They can seek state intervention when a CEC exceeds its brief and even go to court in search of relief. State law should make it clear that other schools have standing to sue against encroachments even if they are not immediately affected, as a way of stabilizing the rules under which all operate. CEOs will also have authority, as explained above, to seek state intervention if the CEC that employs them refuses to close consistently low-performing schools or tries to close schools that do not meet the announced criteria.

Thus, there are ways to discourage CECs from overreaching, but none of them are self-enforcing. Schools and CEOs must be prepared to defend the legal basis of the system.

WHAT IF THE CEO IS NEGLIGENT OR INCOMPETENT?
As described above, the CEC can terminate a CEO for cause or petition the state for a waiver in order to fire a CEO before her term is complete. The state (the governor or state superintendent) would then be positioned to judge whether the conflict between the CEC and CEO was based on one or the other party's unwillingness to take aggressive action on behalf of children in unproductive schools. A CEC requesting a waiver against a do-nothing CEO would probably prevail.

This arrangement provides a way of breaking stalemates between the CEO and CEC. But because requesting a waiver involves risks for both parties (since a CEC that was denied a waiver would have even less leverage over the CEO than before), it also creates incentives for them to work out their differences without involving the state.

WHAT IF SOME SCHOOL PROVIDERS CAPTURE THE CEC?

Jeffrey Henig has pointed out that school operators can be in favor of open markets when they are trying to get a contract or charter, but once they are in they can try to "pull up the drawbridge" to prevent competition.[17] Further, under the constitutional system, school providers can have the same incentive to influence CEC elections that teachers unions now have to elect friendly school board members.[18]

Providers who want to compete in a locality should want to oppose such tactics. However, customer allocation (acceptance that provider X dominates in one locality, provider Y in another) is too common to ignore. Apparent competitors might prefer to accept a given provider's dominance in one locality—that is, "divide and conquer."

Aside from citizen vigilance and countercampaigning by the CEO, the only barriers against this abuse are at the state level. The state can prohibit gifts and campaign contributions from school providers to CEC candidates and can analyze patterns of contracting to identify sweetheart arrangements. It can also intervene by decertifying a CEC in cases where weak schools are left open and competitors are spurned.

HOW WILL THE CEC RELATE TO INDEPENDENT CHARTER AUTHORIZERS?

Many states have empowered entities other than local school boards to authorize charter schools. Such mechanisms have been important under current governance arrangements because many local boards remain highly resistant and, often, openly hostile toward new school providers and strongly favor the schools they operate over any others.

Under a constitutional governance scheme, such problems are unlikely to persist. However, competition among authorizers might still bring some benefits, especially if a locality unnecessarily excludes certain types of schools or providers.

In a system with multiple authorizers, the local CEC will retain the final responsibility to ensure that a good school is available to every child. It can pursue this responsibility in many ways, including cooperation with other authorizers, who might take responsibility for overseeing schools of a particular type or in a specific neighborhood. There is precedent, in New York City and elsewhere, for districts to collaborate with independent charter authorizers, who develop new options and seek to place charter schools where they are most needed.

But a multiple-authorizer arrangement is not without administrative, legal, and political costs under a constitutional system. By design, it blurs accountability for outcomes in a given geographic area. With proper state oversight, including decertification of lax authorizers, some of these hazards may be avoided. This might prove difficult in states like Ohio, where weak authorizers and well-organized school providers have their defenders in the state legislature. Governors and others who favor a constitutional governance system will have to judge whether it is best to put all public schools under a single oversight structure or to retain a more competitive, but also more complicated, system of governance.

SHOULD ALL LOCALITIES BE REQUIRED TO ADOPT THE
CONSTITUTIONAL SYSTEM?

Large cities have the greatest pools of human and organizational capital and are therefore the most likely to benefit from a governance system that is open to new providers and ideas. That is why the portfolio strategy—which can be considered a precursor to constitutional governance but is surely not the same thing— has emerged first in metropolitan cities. However, suburban ring cities and smaller cities also have many assets on the sideline and might benefit from a more open form of educational governance.

State laws establishing the constitutional system are most likely to do so a step at a time. A state might enact the laws underlying constitutional governance but treat them as an option for either the state or localities to exercise. A state could make the new governance mandatory in larger localities with consistently low performance, including those already undergoing state or mayoral takeover or in financial bankruptcy. It could also define financial or academic standards under which additional localities could be required to adopt the new governance. State law could also set a date by which all localities must adopt the new governance. Alternatively it could allow additional localities (those not required to adopt constitutional governance) to put it in place voluntarily. Routes to voluntary adoption could include

- a popular vote requested by citizens via the initiative process; or
- a popular vote requested by the mayor, a majority of the city council, and at least one member of the local school board.

These provisions would mean that a state could have localities with two different governance systems.[19] Of course, future legislators could decide to make constitutional governance mandatory everywhere.

WILL THE PUBLIC FORUM PROVIDED BY TRADITIONAL SCHOOL BOARDS DISAPPEAR?

Traditional school boards can make decisions about almost any aspect of local schooling and provide forums for citizens who have something to say on virtually any topic. Boards can also hear almost any complaint and can intervene, either as a body or individually, in conflicts involving educators, students, and parents. Board members influence administrative decisions even in cases where a board majority would not choose to act. Administrators would rather accommodate them than risk board action whether on the matter at hand or on some other topic.

The constitutional system takes many issues off the CEC agenda entirely. It therefore makes CEC meetings less attractive as a forum for people who are passionate or aggrieved. It also strictly limits the authority of the CEC over central office employees, principals, and teachers.

People with specific grievances about teachers or principals will have to take their issues to the school first and then either to the local ombudsman or to government agencies designed to investigate complaints with a basis in law. The CEC will not have the power to intervene directly, although it could include the number and severity of complaints against a school in its criteria for closure. The CEC will not have the power to do much in response to those with more global issues—for example, for or against phonics or inclusion or exclusion of art, ethnic studies, or history. Those issues can still be argued out in lecture series, legislatures, courts, or in elections for general government, but they will not have a natural place in the deliberations of a CEC.

Whether this is a good or bad result of constitutional governance depends on how much one values what is excluded and what is gained. Eva Gold and colleagues argue that limiting deliberation around schooling and creating a system of schools of choice weakens community ties and makes it more difficult to mobilize people on issues of common interest.[20] Activists who use traditional school board deliberations to publicize positions and build coalitions for broader action might, in theory, be set back. No one has investigated whether activists who use school board meetings as a public forum are particularly effective subsequently. Clearly, such deliberations have symbolic value, giving public recognition to a group or cause that otherwise feels impotent. Groups that gain seats on school boards or take prominent parts in board deliberations seem to be effective in getting their members heard by the school district, but there is no evidence either way on whether students gain as a result.[21] But unbounded deliberations also come at some cost of confusion about the school board's role and possibly flare-ups that might not otherwise occur.

On the gain side, narrowing the public agenda ensures that CEC members can focus on issues they can do something about. As discussed above, the narrower powers of CEC members are less likely to attract candidates who see school politics as a stepping-stone to a broader political career. Similarly, activists with agendas outside education are likely to abandon CEC meetings for other forums.

Conclusion

This chapter shows how constitutional governance would work at the local level. Although it does not focus on the roles of the state government, courts, the federal government, or political organizations, this chapter has had to refer frequently to them. The next chapter shows in detail what roles those other entities will play in constitutional governance, how their powers will be limited, and how they will check and balance the work of CECs.

4

Checks and Balances: The Roles of Other Entities

A constitutionally limited governance system starts with a CEC with important but strictly limited powers. But it does not end there. The system also involves new roles and constraints for other entities, some governmental and some private. Other government agencies—the state and federal government and the courts, have important new roles to play, both in supporting schools and in making sure CECs stay within the boundaries set for them by law. Private entitles, including teachers unions, parents, school operators, and providers of support to schools, also play new roles. In some cases state law will define those roles. In other cases they will emerge in practice.

This chapter shows how constitutional governance of K–12 would define and constrain the roles of entities other than the CEC. It also shows how the emergence of new private interests and institutions is likely to change local and state politics in ways that buttress the new governance system. The first part of the chapter focuses on government, and the second part on private entities.

New Roles for High Levels of Government

Constitutional governance requires changes in the roles now played by the state and federal government and by the courts. Some of these changes can be created by state law, but others will happen in the course of the law's implementation.

STATE GOVERNMENT

The framework of constitutional governance will be set by state laws that define and limit the powers of CECs. Those same laws must also ensure that CECs perform their assigned functions diligently and live within the constraints set for them. (Chapter 8 describes those laws and shows how they can be enacted and kept in effect.)

Aside from creating a clear legal framework, the state's role is to hold CECs accountable, either via the state board of education or the state superintendent. No matter how definite the legal delegation of responsibility to a CEC is, its existence must be contingent on performance. Local CECs that do not pay attention to schools that consistently fail to educate children, or let some groups of children go for years without a good schooling option, need to be sanctioned by loss of control of their schools. CECs that exceed their powers by determining who works in schools, taking the control of budgetary and instructional decisions away from school leaders, or arbitrarily favoring one set of school providers over another must also face sanctions.

State legislation could protect children against a negligent local CEC by empowering a state agency—the governor, state superintendent, or a statewide school district—to dismiss a CEC and make new local oversight arrangements. This could be done by holding elections for a new local CEC, redrawing district boundaries, or transferring oversight responsibility to other CECs.[1]

Sanctions against a negligent CEC could be partial (some schools are taken away from the local CEC and assigned to some other entity) or total (the local CEC is disbanded and its work assigned elsewhere, whether to a new CEC that takes its place or to an existing CEC that takes on responsibility for the local schools).

By law states could also create an emergency mechanism. A statewide school district (modeled after the Louisiana Recovery School District) could seize control of unproductive schools (students, buildings, and budgets) and charter them out to new providers. State legislation could allow a local CEO to seek this form of state intervention, as a counter to a local CEC's refusal to act on behalf of students in a weak school.

Reconstituting CECs that fail to fulfill their legal obligations would preserve the geography of local school systems and limit the need for messy transitions from a CEC to some other governance arrangement. Many states already have oversight of local school systems and can disband a local school board for academic or financial bankruptcy.[2] But most states do not use such powers systematically to oversee public education.[3]

State boards of education should also have "constitutionally" defined powers. Like local CECs, state boards and state education agencies (SEAs) would be denied some current powers that lead to arbitrary or shifting mandates. Limitations like those listed below would reduce the overall level of regulation, both of schools' instructional practices and their uses of time, money, and human resources. State boards would be forbidden by law to

- set barriers beyond the BA and a criminal records check to anyone being employed as a teacher or principal,
- set minimum class sizes or seat-time requirements that govern the minutes students must spend on every subject,
- designate particular textbooks for universal use,
- mandate days or hours of school operation,
- mandate curriculum beyond the content of state student performance standards,
- require that every school adopt a standard staffing or administrative structures,
- change data reporting requirements imposed on schools without explaining the need and cost to the state legislature,

- regulate the characteristics of school buildings in a way more pre-scriptive than the normal building code for buildings used by the public,
- constrain the use of state funds provided to schools via earmarks, and
- provide different amounts of funding for children attending cyber versus brick and mortar schools.

As the following chapter on rights, obligations, and enforcement makes clear, both the state board and SEA would have the authority to receive and review districts' and schools' audited financial reports, but they could not, by mandating a specific form of those reports, create an implicit requirement that schools organize themselves or spend money in specific ways.

On the positive side, state board powers should include setting statewide student learning objectives, judging the performance of CECs, and conducting and disseminating evaluations of promising school models. State boards could also order the development and analysis of statewide longitudinal student and school databases, which would then be supervised by SEAs. In order to improve the options available to local districts, state boards could sponsor and SEAs could administer programs to develop new school models, including online and hybrid approaches.

THE FEDERAL GOVERNMENT

Since the passage of the Elementary and Secondary Education Act in 1965, the federal government has been a major source of rules that decrease school leaders' freedom of action and blur the lines of accountability for children's learning.[4] Indeed, while many federal initiatives to encourage higher academic standards and more effective performance-based oversight are well intentioned, too often they rely upon the same types of mandates that have constrained state and district governance systems and bolstered the administrative arms of those agencies.

How can Congress and the U.S. Department of Education be constrained to respect the boundaries set by constitutional governance? Nothing about K–12 education, or the federal system, makes the current set of federal programs and regulatory structures inevitable. The federal government, if it chose, could construct a new role for itself.

The U.S. Department of Education (DOE) could continue providing support for the education of disadvantaged students, the disabled, and other groups in need (e.g., children with limited English proficiency). However, it would do so in ways compatible with constitutional governance, by tying funds to individual students based on their characteristics and allowing states and localities to add these funds to the "backpacks" of beneficiary students. The U.S. government would rightly want proof that its funds truly added to the amount that accompanied beneficiary children, rather than simply supplanting amounts state and localities spent on them. The DOE could also strengthen constitutional governance by threatening to withhold funds from states that did not play their roles in holding CECs accountable.

This implies abandoning federal categorical programs that limit the use of funds for set activities. The federal government can make a continuing contribution to the quality of education for all American children, particularly the poor and disadvantaged, if it rebuilds its role according to these principles:

- Fund the education of beneficiary children by adding funds to their backpacks. Do not fund specific administrative units or employees.
- Make all grants contingent. Funds must follow children to schools; states and CECs must constantly seek better options for children.
- Do not create new categorical programs as problems arise. Instead, attack emergent problems with short-term special-purpose grants.
- Make DOE a provider of ideas, examples, data, and research, not a prescriptive national ministry.

As this is written, the federal role is in flux. The DOE is negotiating waiver packages and performance guarantees with particular states, and many have proposed consolidating federal programs and supporting family choice.[5] Several competing versions of the law reauthorizing the Elementary and Secondary Education Act could be made compatible with constitutional governance. State laws creating constitutional governance at the state and local level would provide assurance that such dramatic changes in the federal role would benefit, not harm, the disadvantaged groups that federal funds traditionally support.

Courts

The courts exist to hear disputes, and no sensible proposal would call for restriction of their jurisdiction. Judges will hear cases and decide them on what they consider relevant legal principles.

The best way to affect what cases will be heard and how decisions are made is to change the law. Constitutional governance will be based on new frameworks of state law and therefore will affect what courts do. Once the law is established, courts can play a role in constitutional governance by hearing complaints against CECs that have exceeded their powers or neglected their duties. Chapter 5 discusses ways that school operators can sue for relief if their local CECs impose excessive constraints, for example, requiring all local schools to adopt a single salary schedule.

Courts will also surely hear and decide two kinds of challenges to constitutional governance. First, groups whose interests are best served by current governance arrangements will claim that the new laws violate state constitutions or protections of voter rights. Second, individuals who think schools have neglected or mistreated them will sue for compensation and also ask that schools be regulated to prevent similar problems.

The next chapter discusses ways of preventing the second kind of case from regulating schools in ways that undermine constitutional governance. This chapter addresses the first question, whether courts will find laws defining the roles of CECs to be in violation of the local-control principles of state constitutions.

The constitutional system challenges a common assumption about local governing bodies, that their powers must not be circumscribed because they derive from local voters. It also creates a new positive definition of a public school, as a school overseen by a local CEC or other state agency, open to any child whose parents choose it, and funded with taxpayer money. This definition represents a change from a much older definition of a public school as a school directly operated by a local school board.

The openendedness of existing school board powers has created confusion about whether they are little legislatures with essentially sovereign power in the geographic area where they operate. School board members, and their close allies in the district central office and teachers union, often talk as if their powers were derived directly from the local voters who elect them and are therefore unlimited. However, in clear legal terms this is not the case: their power is derived from delegation of the state's responsibility for K–12 education.[6]

Contrary to common perception, local boards are not instances of local popular sovereignty at all: they are state agencies.[7] States create local agencies to oversee K–12 education in a defined geographic area. For the most part, states also provide that local oversight boards will be elected. However, the powers local boards have, the geographic areas they oversee, and how board members are selected are determined by the state legislature. Politics aside, there is no legal barrier to states changing local board powers, redrawing area boundaries, or requiring that members be appointed, even by nonlocal entities like the governor.

States prove this point regularly, as they suspend board control to take control of local districts to prevent bankruptcy, assign control to mayors or special masters, or consolidate formerly separate school districts. As attorney Mitchell Price writes,

> In most states, local control is more of a historical, cultural, and political value than a legal mandate. Courts have consistently reiterated that the authority for public education is not a local one, but rather is a central power residing in the legislature, and court decisions abundantly support the preeminence of the state in control of education. Virtually all state constitutions treat public education as a state function, although a handful do grant power over local schools to local boards (e.g., Georgia, Florida, and Colorado, among others).[8]

Courts have shown deference to the principle of local control but typically in cases in which local-control arguments are used by states themselves as a means of resisting new obligations (e.g., equalizing spending between wealthy and poor districts). In other words, local control is primarily a matter of state policy rather than a constraint imposed by federal or state constitutional law on the states' role in education.

Overall, the tradition of local control has not constrained the states' role in education. However, local control remains a powerful value. Political, economic, and educational arguments for local control continue to enjoy support, so it is likely to remain a rallying cry for some.

New Roles for Private Actors

Constitutional government will affect the roles of private actors including school operators, teacher organizations, and families. It will also cause changes in the interest-group structure of local politics, as some nonprofit organizations and for-profit firms are brought into existence or strengthened and others that prospered under traditional governance are weakened. These forces will diversify the set of interests engaged in education and provide incentives for groups to work together to improve the system's effectiveness, much as downtown business coalitions helped combat urban blight in the 1980s and 1990s.[9] This section describes how constitutional governance will affect different private actors and how they in turn will either threaten or buttress it.

SCHOOL OPERATORS

The next chapter discusses the rights and responsibilities of school operators in detail. Briefly, many groups can operate schools, including nonprofits, neighborhood groups, teacher cooperatives, unions, higher education and cultural institutions, sole proprietors, and organizations and businesses created to run multiple schools. All these groups will receive government funds based on enrollment weighted by pupil characteristics. None will get special government subsidies, such as free facilities, unless schools not receiving this benefit are compensated financially. All schools will be assessed on the same student outcomes, compared with the best outcomes attained anywhere with similar students. Schools will control their budgets, hiring, and instructional methods. However, all must be governed by district-wide admissions processes and admit and serve special education students equitably.

TEACHERS AND THEIR UNIONS

As in every other scheme for governing public schools, what is possible depends on the supply of talented people who can help children learn. This means that the governance system must value teachers and make it possible for them to work productively in rewarding situations.

Under the scheme we propose, teachers will work in a much more diverse set of school environments, and teachers' jobs will vary from school to school much more than now. Some teachers will work in traditional schools, while others will integrate their work and that of their students with forms of online instruction. Still others will provide instruction online or via video and electronic links to students.

Any arbitrary restrictions on the supply of teachers, keeping people out of teaching whose skills might be needed by a particular kind of school, would be self-defeating for a state or district. There is no good reason to rule out schools' paying extra for rare skills or exceptional performance. Nor is there a justification for blocking the employment of teachers who might have advanced education in subjects like mathematics, science, literature, logic, communications, or computer science but lack training in standard teaching methods. The skills schools will need, and how they will be found and developed, must be open to evidence, not prescribed by regulation.

There is real uncertainty about whether a diverse supply of schools can attract enough of the skilled people they will need. It is likely that schools will be forced to innovate in teacher compensation and working conditions to attract the kinds of people they require. More conventional schools might be able to use pay scales similar to those available to teachers today. Others might need to pay much more for teachers with unusual or in-demand skills; to do this they might need to expand the numbers of students such individuals teach via online or video methods or employ such teachers only part time. The way some private high schools employ science and math teachers—hiring college faculty or advanced graduate students in the sciences to teach only a few hours each week at a high hourly rate—is one example of how this might be done. Such schools might also employ lower salaried individuals who have sustained contact with small groups of students and work in ways analogous to university laboratory and teaching assistants.

In most states teachers will always have the right to form bargaining units, demand union elections, and bargain. However, collective bargaining that constrains all schools in a locality is not consistent with a governance system in which schools make their own hiring decisions, decide how to organize themselves, assess the value of employees and set pay. One approach to dealing with these issues is to limit collective bargaining to the school level, or in the case of management organizations that operate several schools locally, at that level. In short, whatever organization hires, assigns, and pays teachers will be the appropriate bargaining unit for teacher unions to try to organize. Individual schools or CMOs could be union shops or not, at the option of their teachers. Unions might also choose to sponsor benefit and retirement plans for their members by bargaining with insurers.

Because the local CEC would not be party to employer-level labor agreements, its funding and school assessment policies could take no account of a school's status as a union shop. Thus, the district would not pay extra to a school whose labor contract led to a higher wage bill than the school could pay. Teachers, unions, and school managers would share an interest in avoiding making their school unsustainable. The local CEC must retain the freedom to take students and funding away from a school or

CMO that cannot manage its labor relations, is unable to motivate or replace ineffective employees, or makes unsustainable salary commitments.

In general, modes of teacher employment will be a major factor in any school's or group of schools' approach to instruction. Teachers who have needed skills and reputations for working productively in particular working environments will have a great deal of market power. Their incomes will be constrained only by what schools can afford to pay. Thus at last teachers can become what Linda Darling-Hammond and other analysts of the teaching force have long advocated—professionals who like physicians are able to control their conditions of work.[10] On the other side of the coin, there will not be secure places for teachers who do not develop reputations and skills and cannot adapt—as other professionals must—to constantly evolving demands, methods, uses or technology, and ways of organizing work.

FAMILIES

Parents and guardians constrain and inform local CEC actions. CECs can approve a set of schools to operate in their localities, but schools can survive only if parents send their children, and thus the money in the children's backpacks, to them.[11]

Families function as a constraint on a CEC's efforts to cull weak schools and create more promising ones. As we have shown elsewhere,[12] families often resist closure of schools that have become neighborhood fixtures and can resent the implied message in a school closure that parents have been sending their children to a bad school. As agents of the state, local CECs have a responsibility to prevent children from going to schools that cannot prepare them for adult life, so some conflict with parents is likely. It is not clear whether these conflicts will be as virulent under the new governance system as they have been in traditional districts, where teachers unions lead opposition to school closings on behalf of the incumbent teachers and to avoid precedents that undermine collective bargaining agreements. However, it is clear that local CECs will have to make the case for school openings and closings by setting clear consistent criteria and make sure parents see how their children will benefit from CEC actions. Local CECs will also hear complaints from parents about particular schools, teachers, school buildings, and so on. To the degree possible these need to be sent back to the school for resolution, with the understanding that parents who cannot be satisfied can get help finding a more congenial placement. For parents who have been defrauded or abused, the CEC could refer complaints to the appropriate legal jurisdiction, for example, the local police or state financial auditor. The CEC could invest in an ombudsman who could arbitrate parent claims, negotiate solutions including new placements for students, and identify problems serious enough to justify an investigation into whether a school should lose its charter.

INTEREST GROUPS

The constitutional governance system will encourage the development of support groups—principals, school providers, and support organizations—as well as weaken opponents—teachers unions and professional associations representing central office bureaucrats. The remodeling of politics around new governance realities is a kind of "policy feedback" in which changes to how authority and resources are allocated to remake the political landscape. Consider the following:

Principals, empowered by new rules around school autonomy and fewer compliance mandates, will have strong incentives to resist efforts to regulate the responsibilities of school leadership.
New school providers—networks of independent school heads and coalitions of charter management organizations or online instruction providers—will emerge as a powerful force as the marketplace for schools diversifies and opens up. These groups will have strong interests in sustaining the new governance system, and they might supplant teachers unions as the most important sources of advocacy for high rates of per-pupil spending.
Independent organizations that provide services to schools— everything from teacher training to transportation, accounting,

legal services, and facilities—are likely to become strong support-ers of the new regime. As money and functions are moved from district central offices into the hands of schools, these providers will experience enhanced demand for their services, so existing or-ganizations will grow, and new organizations will enter the market. Like school providers, these organizations will resist any return to central control of resources and bureaucratic provision of services.

Although interest organizations that thrived under the old governance structure will not go away, they will be weakened. The teachers union will no longer be authorized to negotiate district-wide pay and placement schemes. They will face tough competition in the political marketplace from the principals who value their autonomy over hiring, parents who value school choice, new school providers who are wary of collective bargain-ing, and school support organizations who operate in contrast to centralized professional development apparatuses.

How fiercely groups that prefer traditional governance will react to these changes is not clear. Unions, of course, could con-tinue to represent teachers, albeit teachers employed by indi-vidual schools or school networks. They would still favor higher public spending on K–12, assuming that increases will lead to teacher salary increases, and call attention to circumstances that interfere with effective teaching or drive out good teachers. In other words, they could become akin to the American Medical Association—advancing the cause of teachers but not through restrictive rules that run counter to school autonomy. This fits the vision of professionalized unions offered by Charles Kerchner and his colleagues.[13]

Local school boards will be replaced by CECs elected to work under the new constitutional governance scheme. They will face different pressures from organized groups and parents than did traditional school board members and have less incentive to channel benefits toward particular groups. Changing the tim-ing of board elections to maximize voter turnout could intensify these new, more pluralistic pressures on boards.

Some groups' support or opposition to the new governance

scheme will depend on results for particular children. Although parents and advocates for special needs children are generally dissatisfied with the services provided by the traditional public school system, support for a new system will depend on whether it can result in better organized and more effective arrangements. These could come from risk sharing and service pooling agreements among independent public schools, school-supported clearinghouses for families seeking special education services, and best-practice sharing among schools about how to target early interventions. However, schools' efforts to avoid accepting special needs students or to pass hard-to-serve children on to other providers until one school is forced to deal with a student with complex needs can quickly discredit the new governance system in these parents' eyes.

Findings from cities implementing district-wide choice programs reveal that parents are often more satisfied with their schools when enabled with choice.[14] Other research suggests that parental choice programs increase political engagement with education and that parents exercising choice are more, not less, likely to talk with other parents about schools, join the PTA, and trust teachers.[15] These are positive signs that parents can become a natural ally of governance reform.

Conclusion: Constitutional Governance as "Good" Governance

Table 4.1 reviews the proposed constitutional system in light of the five criteria presented in chapter 2. Based on its principles, constitutional governance can meet all the criteria. But, of course, no governance system is proof against negligence or failure of key actors to use their powers for the benefit of children. The current governance system might also fit these criteria, if it lived up to its aspirations. Unfortunately, encrustation of rules and processes, many of them created through interest advocacy, protects key adult group interests regardless of the consequences for children.

The constitutional governance system is designed to serve

TABLE 4.1 The constitutional system meets our five criteria

Criterion	How the constitutional governance system meets it
Efficient	Schools are empowered to do their best work with substantial autonomy. In return, they face a combination of strictly defined revenues, competition, and the possibility of being closed if they are ineffective. This creates strong incentives for continuous improvement, seeking the best ideas available and eliminating ineffective aspects of the school program. States and districts could use a cost-effectiveness framework to identify the most and least productive schools and improve (or close) the least.
Equitable	Weighted student funding would equalize resources according to need and give schools incentives to enroll disadvantaged students. The CEC's oversight function would also guarantee that efforts to find more effective providers would focus on low-performing schools. Special education and equitable admissions guarantees would continue.
Transparent	Flow of public dollars would be driven only by enrollment. Schools could be required to report expenditures annually, and these would be included in the state's longitudinal database.
Accountable	Parties held responsible for children's learning would have the freedom of action to provide students what they need. Thus, rewards (greater enrollment, opportunities to expand) or penalties (shrinking or closure) would be logical consequences of performance. CECs would face sanctions including replacement if they indulged ineffective schools. Lower levels of government, like the CEC, are held accountable for their actions by higher levels of government, including the state and federal governments.
Democratic	Ultimately responsive to voters but not necessarily controlled in detail via constant interest bargaining and casework

public purposes. That does not mean, however, that it cannot be corrupted. Any system run by humans will depend on thoughtfulness, diligence, and leadership. Future chapters will discuss the ways this system can go wrong—particularly how providers and other actors working in their own self-interest can fail to do the best for children—and how to prevent it.

5

School Rights and Obligations

In a constitutional governance system, every school's existence will depend on enrollment choices made by parents and on performance sufficient to avoid being closed by the CEC. But with great responsibility must come great freedom. Schools can only use methods, time, and money in new ways and for greater effect if they are given both the incentive *and* the freedom to do so.

How can a system be designed to provide school leaders real and sustainable autonomy? Just as the U.S. Constitutional framework expressly limited government and established citizen rights, effective K–12 governance must do more than describe how government will oversee schools. It must also say what freedoms schools will have and how far those freedoms extend. This chapter shows how clarity about the rights and obligations of schools can help both enhance school autonomy in the short run and stabilize it over time.

The Limits of School Autonomy

Past attempts to empower school leaders including site-based management reforms of the 1980s and early 1990s were abandoned in most localities.[1] Yet such efforts never fully empowered schools. School leaders were not allowed to make new uses of dollars or staff.[2] School leaders were free to use dollars any way they wanted to as long as they continued paying their current teaching staff, a requirement that used up virtually all the money.

The charter school movement has been plagued by similar confusions about schools' freedom of action. Charters have the advantage of a distinctive legal status, freeing them from district collective bargaining agreements and providing them with greater budgetary freedom. Yet many still live with uncertainty about whether charter authorizers will keep their promises and on what basis a school will ultimately be judged.

Ambiguity about school freedoms and obligations can make educators timid. It can also confuse parents, lead advocacy groups to make demands schools cannot meet, and generate lawsuits, all of which can reintroduce counterproductive constraints.

As Philip Howard put it, "we seem to have achieved the worst of both worlds: a system of regulation that does too much while it also does too little."[3] As the Organization for Economic Cooperation and Development reported following a review of regulatory reforms in member countries, "Too often, legislators issue laws as symbolic public action, rather than as practical solutions to real problems. Regulatory inflation erodes the effectiveness of all regulations, disproportionately hurts [small providers] and expands scope for misuse of administrative discretion and corruption."[4]

The use of contracts (or, in states with such laws, charters) between schools and CECs is the key to defining and limiting school autonomy. Informal agreements are not enough because their meaning can drift and one party's actions can invalidate them. Formal contracts between CECs and schools provide a firmer legal basis for both specifying and enforcing schools' rights and obligations. Contracts can prevent either the school or the CEC from unilaterally adding burdens or reneging on commitments. Either side should have rights in the case of a violation of contract terms and expect to be compensated for the other's failure to perform.

Use of real contracts implies that either side can enforce the other's obligations by reference to a court, which can award damages to the injured party. Of course it also means that school operators need to be prepared to enforce their rights under contracts and not to accept harmful changes rather than risk government overseers' displeasure.

Schools' Rights

A constitutional governance system would includes a "school bill of rights," which is outlined in Table 5.1. It would guarantee that during the term of a school's contract, the CEC would not unilaterally change crucial arrangements like the basis on which schools are paid, make late payments, fail to provide promised government facilities and services, or impose new burdens like additional reporting requirements. The CEC can try to add provisions to the contract the next time it is reviewed, but of course a school can negotiate or withdraw if the government's terms are unworkable. Good school providers will always be in short supply and will have opportunities in neighboring districts.

This bill of rights would apply to any publicly funded school, whether nonprofit or for profit and whether it delivered instruc-

TABLE 5.1 A school bill of rights

		Remedies available to schools		
Schools are protected from	1 year's notice	Regulatory cost analysis, public comment, and review by an independent body	Financial compensation	Withdrawal without penalty
Late or partial payments			X	
District failure to provide promised facilities or services			X	X
Changes in attendance boundaries or admissions rules	X	X		X
New reporting requirements	X	X		
New rules about student services	X	X		
New rules about hiring	X	X		X

tion in person or via technology. If a school served its students effectively, it would not matter whether some funding goes to profit or is used to invest in development of new methods or whether the school does or does not pay rent or provides instruction in person or online. Students would receive public funds in order to produce results, not to pay for particular cost structures.

As outlined, schools would have a variety of enforcement mechanisms available to them to ensure that the CEC could not change the rules midgame. Schools in the middle of their contracts would be entitled to at least one year's notice before some new obligations are imposed, could comment on proposed rules changes, propose alternatives, and demand that new rules be reviewed by an independent body, for example, the state department of education. In some cases, schools could claim compensation for costs imposed and seek damages in court. In other cases, the school has the option of terminating its agreement with the local board (e.g., saying it will no longer operate in the city or district once a new regulation is imposed or seeking a charter from an independent authorizer to keep the school open) without penalty.

Where schools are entitled to seek financial compensation (as specified in table 5.1), they must be able to appeal to some entity other than the CEC. Schools should be free to use local and state courts, but it might be less burdensome for all concerned if the state education agency employed an administrative law judge or hearing officer, who would be able to standardize the interpretations of law and awards of compensation statewide and to build up a body of precedents. The very existence of this avenue of appeal would probably deter CECs from some encroachments on schools' freedom of action.

This bill of rights does not absolutely prevent the erosion of school autonomy, but it deters it and forces government overseers to justify their actions and to bear the costs of failure to deliver on their side of the bargain. When constitutional governance is fully operational, a local CEC would not have the option of changing the rules in order to drive out an independently operated school for reasons other than those related to its performance and legal

BOX 5.1 On data demands

State and federal agencies that oversee schools must ultimately report something to higher governments and legislatures. Predictable reports would include numbers and demographic characteristics of students— who applied, who was admitted, how many stayed to graduation, how many dropped out, and how many were expelled—and of teachers and administrators. Agencies also need some form of financial reporting. Unfortunately, school authorizers seldom if ever think these needs through in advance. Charter and voucher schools consequently receive unanticipated data requests when the authorizers are asked a question or forced to answer a criticism. These requests often require emergency staff work and divert energy from the normal work of the school.

Unanticipated data requests are especially common for charter schools created by school districts. District officials are accustomed to making demands on district-operated schools and generally have not thought ahead about what they need from charter schools.* Compared with independent charter authorizers, districts are subject to a great deal more press scrutiny and must provide data-based responses to more charges and accusations.

Without judging whether particular data requests are necessary, many data demands are easy to anticipate and therefore should be defined in advance—about what data are required, in which form, and in what schedule—so schools can organize their work in anticipation. For example, contract renewals occur at regular intervals, and because of performance problems, some schools will be required to provide more information than others.

School contracts could specify the regular reporting requirements that all schools must meet and then provide a pricing structure, specifying what the district must pay a school to get information beyond what was specified. This formalization would complicate the negotiation of charter renewal agreements, but it is consistent with good faith negotiations.

---

* Central Michigan University, a well-organized independent charter authorizer, discovered that no one in the Michigan Department of Education could tell them all the data a charter school must report or when. The authorizer took the initiative to identify all the reports charter schools would be required to make, provided all the schools it chartered with a complete listing of content and timing, and also provided schools with the appropriate forms on computer disks. After the first year in which this was done, the authorizer also provided schools with filled-in forms from the previous year, which schools simply had to update.

obligations under its contract. If a school operator abandoned its contract rather than continue under the new rules, the CEC would need to attract another independent party to serve the students. Knowing this, CECs will think twice before taking an action that might drive out a functioning school operator. Local CECs with bad reputations for meddling in schools will experience difficulty attracting new operators and could lose control of those schools to the state.

Schools' Obligations

There is no such thing as public funding without strings. That is a fact of life, not something to be regretted: after all, taxpayers part with their money expecting it will be used with some care and for a public purpose. Parents also give up control of their children to schools, and they need to be confident that the children's time is being used well. Student testing and fiscal and enrollment reporting come with the territory.

One of the chief oversight challenges in our current governance system is a poor specification of the obligations of school providers and overseers. Clarifying obligations then is a significant part of creating a constitutional governance system.

Table 5.2 summarizes the respective obligations of CECs and the providers themselves. By assigning risk to one party or the other, it says who must make sure that various aspects of a partnership truly work to the benefit of children.

School providers and government overseers must be very clear about how three kinds of challenges are to be met:

- demands related to student rights;
- demands related to poor performance; and
- regulations imposed owing to scandals and crises and, less commonly, to criminal behavior.

The next short sections explain the problems these demands can cause when they are unanticipated and how they can be managed in ways that are less disruptive.

TABLE 5.2 Who is responsible for what

Risk	Borne by local CEC	Borne by school provider
Low enrollment		X
Inability to find teachers		X
Late or partial payments to school	X	
School inability to meet financial obligations despite receiving all payments		X
School said it could get a facility but cannot		X
Disruption, conflict within the school		X
Changes in district attendance boundaries	X	
Failure to reach enrollment goals for disadvantaged		X
Frequent departure of teachers		X
Change in demographics, needs of students enrolled		X
New compliance or reporting requirements	X	
Availability of promised government-provided services	X	
Low student performance		X
Loss of promised state or federal funds	X	
Loss of funds expected to be raised by the school		X

STUDENT RIGHTS

Most of the policies and court orders about fair admissions, student due process rights, rights of the disabled, and language-minority children were established before the growth of chartering and state voucher programs. There was no chance the same requirements would not be imposed on these new forms of publicly funded schooling. Yet both charter and voucher laws were enacted with at best vague references to such issues.

Many charter school operators started off thinking they had no practical constraints, but experience has shown that they were wrong.[5] People who think a school has denied someone rights guaranteed by the Constitution or civil rights statutes can ask courts to intervene; court orders can become precedents that constrain everyone in unexpected ways. If some publicly funded schools discriminate against students or teachers on the basis of age, sex, or disabling condition, constraints on all schools are sure to follow.

Charter schools operators' assumption that they could set

admissions requirements—discouraging applications from students with chaotic families, running lotteries early to get the best pool of applicants, encouraging some students to leave the school but refusing to accept new students midyear, and limiting services to special education students—has caused political firestorms and litigation.[6]

The fact that these issues are still unresolved in New York City is a major liability to the reform movement there. Charter schools have accepted a uniform admissions process for all schools, but many are still refusing to accept students who arrive in the city or transfer schools in midyear (locally called "over-the-counter students"). This has forced regular district schools to take in all the difficult cases that arrive after schools open and reinforces resistance to charters as inequitable and playing by a different set of rules and obligations. This arrangement will surely lead to new regulation of charters, and it has already imposed great political costs.

In New Orleans, charter school operators have now accepted government-run admissions processes that give every applicant an equal chance at entry to a charter school and expects that charters will be open to midyear admissions. Owing to a Southern Poverty Law Center civil rights lawsuit about services to disabled children, New Orleans charters are now admitting students regardless of disability status. They are also forming service delivery consortia and financial risk pools to ensure that students needing expensive programs can be served. Other localities are trying to learn from their experience.

Greater anticipation of problems related to student rights and clear specification of school providers' service obligations to students and families can help to prevent poorly planned and executed regulations. Compare, for example, the positive example of New Orleans' emerging special education services system, in which charters pool funding and build complementary special education capacities, with the suggestion that every charter be forced to enroll and serve a specific number of special education students.[7]

POOR PERFORMANCE

Under the current regime, laws like the No Child Left Behind Act (NCLB) as well as state-level accountability systems make demands on schools related to poor performance. With NCLB, poor performance over successive years resulted in sanctions—in the form of both mandated services and public school choice requirements. State-level accountability systems were layered onto the federal requirements, sometimes resulting in school takeovers but more often resulting in interventions that might include district-assisted planning processes, mandated curriculum changes, and so on.

The use of mandates has not proven very effective. It is a great irony that the reform movement, which has made its name by knocking restrictive collective bargaining agreements, has embraced mandates—including teacher evaluation measures, school turnaround strategies, curriculum, and the like—approaches that are just as harmful to school autonomy. Neither approach works because each one fails to respect the expertise and position of school leaders and their staff in establishing the direction of their schools. Under a constitutional governance system, such restrictions on use of strategy, staff, time, or money would not be permitted. It would not matter whether proposed restrictions came from the political left, teacher unions, or reformers eager to remake all schools in a particular way.

States or CECs might vary on how they choose to measure performance (e.g., student test scores, school culture, parental support), what adequate growth looks like (including variation among student subgroups), and what consequences stem from poor performance over time. The key point is that self-governing schools have at their disposal all the resources required to make improvement. They can hire new staff, purchase a new curriculum, contract for school turnaround services, and so on. But the onus to do these things is on the leadership of the school, not the district, not the state, and certainly not the federal government.

IMPROPER OR CRIMINAL BEHAVIOR

No matter how good a job is done anticipating problems related to student rights, new ones will arise. These can be caused by conflicts among or between parents and teachers, deviant or insane behavior by school staff, and theft or misuse of public funds. Such events can lead to overreactions that institutionalize new, burdensome rules, whether in an attempt to prevent any such event from happening again or to symbolize concern. Policies or court orders crafted in such situations are rarely the result of careful, well-thought and executed policy making.

The adage "bad cases make bad law" applies here. Panicky action by legislators or administrators or court cases that lead to burdensome new rules that have perverse unintended consequences can result in good programs or school providers being shut out as a result of the careless actions of a few. Louisiana's newly enacted voucher law, for example, provides few definitions of school eligibility and financial reporting requirements and offers vouchers to religious schools that probably will not pass Constitutional tests on separation of church and state.[8] In such cases, the lack of rules in the short run actually increases the likelihood of growing regulatory burden in the long run.

But no amount of anticipation can completely prevent the scandals caused by personal misbehavior. Despite personal background checks and clear legal and professional norms, for example, a tiny number of teachers will enter inappropriate relationships with students. Similarly, transfers of public funds to independent school operators will ultimately lead to rare but devastating instances of deceptive and even criminal misuse of funds. Money once transferred to a school under a charter or voucher program is almost impossible to recover, so both the students on whose behalf the money was to be spent and the taxpayers who provided it lose. Public agencies that authorize charters are increasingly focused on the need to assess the financial competence of a potential school operator, but they are much less good at day-to-day financial oversight. They lack the data, analytical tools, and staffing required for careful analysis of school spending.

One partial remedy is to simplify oversight rules so as to render the system more focused and effective. Bruno Manno proposed that all publicly funded schools follow a common set of accounting standards, which would be specified in their original charters or contracts.[9] This would eliminate surprises, simplify oversight, and reduce the accounting and reporting burdens on school leaders, since private firms could offer fee-based standard services to many schools.

However, when it comes to theft, embezzlement, personal misconduct, and abuse of power, CECs and charter authorizers are not likely to develop investigative powers and forensic accounting capacities. Once violations occur, the simplest option is for CECs and other authorizers to treat them as problems to be addressed by regular law enforcement agencies.

This would insulate entities charged with overseeing the performance of school providers from technical burdens they are not competent or funded to carry. It would also lead to clear adjudication of charges and precedents to guide school leaders' actions. Finally, it could protect school leaders from amateur snooping and case making.

Eliminating Action "for the Convenience of the Government"[10]

As noted in the first chapter, the hard wiring of rules and enforcement mechanisms is only part of governance. Governance also creates attitudes and habits that can constrain practice even more than is intended. State and federal officials continually claim that they do not intend school and district leaders to be as bound up and unable to adapt as school heads feel they are. Of course, school and district leaders are driven to self-protective behavior by threats and feints of oversight bureaus and compliance coordinators who use the rules to enhance their own power. In the end, in as earnest an enterprise as schooling, people take the rules—those written down and those only thought to apply—seriously.

The kind of governance system we describe, including the extra elements discussed early in this chapter, will ultimately transform the culture of public education, replacing a preoccupation with compliance and responsibility avoidance with one focused on performance and aggressive pursuit of new ideas. It will do this in part by attracting people with backgrounds in competitive sectors including business and the professions.

The new system will also slowly change the attitudes of traditional educators who choose to stay. On both sides of the Atlantic (in English primary and secondary schools and the hundreds of newly autonomous schools in New York City), school heads who originally resisted taking full responsibility for their schools' uses of time, talent, and money quickly came to see the advantages. Now, English and New York school heads cherish their freedom of action on grounds that it gives them a chance to raise student performance.[11] Similarly, in New Orleans, the opportunities for innovation and operational control have attracted principals from outer cities and other professions, who previously would not have considered working in that city's schools.

These cultural changes will only continue, however, if local boards and other government agencies rigorously stay within their boundaries. This can be challenging, especially in a legal system that often allows government to change its mind and terminate contractual relationships (e.g., charters and contracts with other schools of choice) at its convenience. When government agencies assume that they can change the rules of the game at will, school leaders know that any statement of school rights and obligations is temporary and unreliable. Under these circumstances, freedoms are seen as expressions of grace and favor, not as rights. Educators have a strong incentive to develop personal relationships with government officials and to store up credits by deferring to government officials' preferences—in effect by returning to a patronage-driven mentality.

How can we overcome the presumption that local boards and other agencies can do as they like regardless of the terms of contracts? One answer is to establish by law that local boards can be sued for violations of contracts, especially those listed on the school bill of rights. Government is far less likely to throw its weight around in a sector where courts have proven they will enforce others' rights.

School heads and organizations that manage multiple schools (e.g., charter management organizations) also need to enforce their rights under contracts. That means resisting demands that clearly violate the terms of charters or contracts and the school bill of rights and being willing to sue the government, when it takes unwarranted actions or fails to deliver promised funds, assets, and services.

This will require a change in attitude for charter school heads and multischool networks. These have traditionally either gone along when government changed its tune or withdrawn from situations rather than take the government to court.

Just as a new governance system will require school providers to regulate themselves and one another in order to maintain their independence, so also will it require school providers to defend their turf. This will cost money. Pro-reform foundations, which have also generally preferred to accept rather than confront government encroachment on school freedoms, will need to support some litigation. Schools will not have to prevail many times in lawsuits for the culture of government to change.

Conclusion

By assigning rights and obligations, a constitutional governance system provides the authority and incentives for actors to carry out their respective responsibilities. Ideas like school bills of rights and risk allocation between CECs and school providers are indispensable aspects of a good governance system. Chapter 8 will have more to say about how to institutionalize good governance and manage the inevitable implementation challenges.

6

Reimagining the Central Office

Today, all but the smallest school districts have some form of central bureaucracy. In larger districts built on the traditional model, central office bureaucracies can employ more than half as many people as work in the schools. Of course not all of the money spent on the central office goes for administration. Much of it goes to people who deliver services to schools and for the equipment they use. Central offices provide in-service training for teachers, advice to principals, after-school programs for at-risk students, as well as transportation, food services, warehousing, and facilities management.

Central office activities are often characterized as wasteful and occasionally as corrupt. Those accusations might be true in some cases, but central offices also employ competent people who work hard and provide real help to schools. The changes in central offices that would occur under a constitutional governance system do not stem from moral disapproval. Instead, the central offices change because they must in a system in which school-level personnel control their own resources.

In this chapter, we show there will still be a need for some form of local central office under a constitutional governance system. What this looks like will vary based on local circumstances including the ability of third-party providers to meet the needs of schools that are free to buy what they need. While the specifics differ, there is no doubt that central offices will be considerably leaner than the ones that exist today.

The Knock on Central Offices

Central office functions are the accumulation of years of choices. District administration evolved to accommodate new programs and funding streams from the federal, state, and local governments. It was transformed by court decisions that mandated use of resources, staff, and time. And its size and complexity were increased by the rise of special interests in education—the gifted, special education, neighborhood groups, religious groups, and teacher unions—each of which gained institutional homes in the district bureaucracy as special liaison units were built and new programs created.

The traditional central office is built to

- ensure uniform and faithful implementation of district-wide instructional methods and programs;
- create economies of scale in procurement, service delivery, and administration (e.g., payroll management);
- manage all the hiring, allocate teachers, and administer the district-wide collective bargaining agreement;[1]
- ensure compliance with requirements imposed by civil rights laws, court orders, and federal and state funding programs; and
- negotiate with community groups and school boards to develop district-wide policy.

Because central offices are responsible for so much, they consume relatively large pieces of the governance pie—in terms of decision-making authority and resources. Marguerite Roza's consideration of district resource allocation practices reveals that districts directly manage a significant share of K–12 expenditures (between 24 and 27 percent).[2] This does not include the large number of staff employed and services that are administered centrally but distributed to schools, like instructional aides, special education services, and so on.

Central offices were built to administer a system in which important decisions were made centrally and implemented at the school level.[3] Although schools were expected to differ in some ways, depending on the age of the students served and special characteristics of the student population (e.g., language-minority status), most schools were expected to offer the same approach to instruction and student services. In part because students were normally assigned to schools based on residence, districts tried to avoid the impression that there were big differences among schools in programming.

This move toward greater centralization over time resulted in some schools receiving services they did not need, while others did not receive services they needed.[4] It exacerbated intradistrict funding inequities and increased the concentration of the most experienced and highest paid teachers in the schools that serviced the fewest disadvantaged students.[5] And it imposed a degree of uniformity in instruction and curriculum that reduced the ability of instructional leaders to adapt to the demands of their environment.

While there is good evidence that some central office policies work against (or at least, not toward) greater school effectiveness, prescriptions for reform are all too often based on the faulty logic that the central office is something that should be done away with *altogether*. This is the theme underlying Chubb and Moe's regulated school markets and, more recently, Andy Smarick's prescription for portfolio management. It suggests that centralized administration is virtually never appropriate. But, is that right?

In the private sector, centralized administrative structures—otherwise known as corporate headquarters—are not always objects of scorn. They play important roles in setting strategic objectives, measuring progress, holding middle management accountable for performance, and managing firm-wide communication and recruiting strategies.[6] These functions are aimed at both avoiding loss by setting standards and monitoring subsidiaries as well as creating value across the organization by sharing knowledge and building economies of scale.[7]

Can the central office be redesigned to play similar roles in K–12 governance? We think it can, and in the pages that follow, we show how.

Doing Both More and Less: Prioritizing the Central Office's Work

Under constitutional governance, central offices are designed to provide data for oversight and coordinate service functions to the benefit of autonomous schools. Their chief responsibilities are identifying service providers, setting standards, measuring progress, and judging performance. They will also play roles in managing choice-based enrollment processes, coordinating transportation with enrollment, and developing a talent strategy to attract human capital to the district.

A redesigned central office would not need the staffing and capacity required to hire large numbers of teachers and principals. Nor would it, in a district built on school diversity, choice, and innovation, manage the implementation of district-wide mandates on instruction. Some responsibilities for compliance with civil rights mandates and court orders would remain. But pupil-based funding would virtually eliminate most regulation-rich categorical programs.

A redesigned central office would provide

Leadership—through the CEO, who would act as the public face for the governance system.

Portfolio management—overseeing and managing the district's portfolio of autonomous school providers using school performance data to make recommendations to the CEO and CEC about which schools to maintain in the portfolio and which need to be closed/replaced.

Talent recruitment and management—developing talent pipelines for the district and clearing barriers that might prevent schools from finding the teachers and in some cases principals they need.

Data—tracking data on indicators of school performance and producing a performance review process that is accessible by both the community and school staff.

Communication—communicating school data, enrollment information, and school closure/opening decisions to parents and other stakeholders.

Enrollment—creating a common enrollment system across all local publicly funded schools and managing it to ensure an equitable and fair enrollment process.

Transportation—leading the work that ensures that students get to schools. This may mean providing transportation directly on a fee basis or it may mean releasing funds for schools and supporting schools in finding transportation providers that are quality options for transporting students or arranging for students to ride public transportation. The central office might also create choice zones within the city, so that students would have many options near their homes and not need to travel long distances to school.

Finance—leading implementation of student-based budgeting, making sure schools receive the funding they are entitled to and in the right amounts given enrollment, and performing district-wide audit functions to demonstrate compliance with state and federal law.

These are "core" central office functions and define the basic mission and administrative structure of a remissioned central office. All other possible central office functions are "contingent" because decisions to utilize centrally administered services that are also available elsewhere rest with school-level personnel. Central offices can offer services for professional development, instruction, and curriculum but cannot exclude competition from independent providers that might deliver better service, lower prices, or both.

It is important to note that once a district mandates a use of funds by requiring schools to purchase certain services, it no longer becomes contingent. Contingent, by definition, means that school approval is required for the service to be rendered. Hence, data management is not contingent because performance-based oversight requires a centrally administered data system to guide performance decisions. From this perspective, central office services offered "free" to schools are not free at all: they are purchased by imposing taxes (via the withholding of revenue for central administration) before money is passed on to the schools.

BOX 6.1 The case of facilities management

Facilities management is a special issue that requires additional consideration. On the face of it, facilities management seems to be a clear case in which central management is beneficial, perhaps even necessary given the vagaries of enrollment and school authorization and closure. However, the issue is complicated by two facts. First is that not all schools require the same kinds of facilities, and as a result, facilities must be seen as a real cost to schools—with space being a resource that could, potentially, be flexibly deployed or traded for creative uses of technology. Second is that direct ownership of facilities creates potential conflicts of interest for district leaders, who are responsible for both encouraging innovative schools that might not use facilities in conventional ways yet making sure the facilities they own are fully leased and not losing money.

One challenge this arrangement poses is what to do about school facilities in high-cost urban areas (e.g., downtowns). Districts could choose to provide a facilities' subsidy to such schools based on the difference in fair market value between high rent and other areas. As long as such subsidies are tied to market rates, they need not result in a rush to move downtown.

Services like uniform admissions processes are indispensable and must be performed centrally. But the need for many other traditional central office services, including coaching, professional development, and even janitorial services, will vary from school to school. In a system of autonomous schools, schools need to be able to choose when, whether, in what form, and at what intensity they receive such services. This is impossible if a central office unit can impose taxes and offer services in ways that fit its own preferences and capacities.

HOW THE COMPLIANCE OVERSIGHT ROLE CHANGES

Traditionally, districts have overseen schools based on compliance—a role that largely has involved districts translating demands from federal, state, and district overseers into specific requirements that schools must satisfy. Some of these, such as "adequate yearly progress" requirements associated with NCLB, are closely connected to performance evaluation. But most revolve around specific reporting demands to ensure that funds are used in compliance with regulatory requirements. It is unlikely that such compliance monitoring can be eliminated entirely. Public education is a publicly funded enterprise that demands some stewardship of funds and accountability for how those funds are used. However, it will be reduced dramatically as federal and state grant programs are consolidated, simplified, and transformed into weights within general pupil-based funding formulas (see chapters 5 and 7 on student-weighted funding and its implications for federal programs).

Along with these roles, however, the district central office must build new oversight capacities to better manage school performance. Whereas traditional central offices managed school performance primarily by mandating the use of funds and staff, a reformed central office must develop the tools of "steering," not "rowing," to use the words of David Osbourne and Ted Gaebler.[8] As schools gain more flexibility and autonomy, they also gain greater responsibility for the results they produce, and district oversight shifts from one oriented to *what schools do* to *what outcomes they produce.*

This changes the nature of oversight work considerably. As long as districts control decisions about how schools are organized, whom they employ, and how they use time and money, it remains difficult to hold schools accountable for outcomes. As Helen Ladd observes, "[T]he main problem with the coach[ing] model is that once inspectors have provided guidance, it is difficult for them subsequently to criticize the school when following the guidance or assistance has not led to the desired results."[9] Consistent with this observation, New Zealand and the Netherlands have both made explicit attempts to separate the "inspectorate" functions aimed at overseeing and managing school quality from assistance functions aimed at improving quality. As Malcolm Sparrow observes about other public sector agencies, the core mission of oversight providers—the Environmental

Protection Agency, the Securities and Exchange Commission, or the Occupational Health Service Agency—involves the delivery of obligations, not services.[10]

Building capacity to oversee schools on the basis of performance data including student outcomes and enrollment patterns will require investments in new data systems capable of tracking outcomes on an individual (and longitudinal) basis. Because choice allows students to move among schools, outcomes data must *follow* students over time, not just be kept as school-wide averages. The district must analyze these data to assess whether students in a particular school are learning at a rate that will allow them to move on to the next level of education on time. The analysis results need to be timely enough and of high enough quality to support decisions about whether to continue supporting a school or a stop allowing students to enroll in it. Such changes will require new staff with different skill sets and bases of expertise than are traditionally in use in central offices.

CAPACITY BUILDING FOR A SYSTEM OF DIVERSE SCHOOLS
While districts will no longer be constructed primarily as service delivery institutions, schools will still need support, especially during the transition to autonomy. Who will take on the job of building capacity so schools can get help when they need it?

Constitutional governance would lead to a system of diverse schools, not one where standardization of capacity-building methods or materials is plausible or desirable. It also contemplates further diversification of teacher roles, as some schools will enable teachers to use technology extensively, while others will not. Thus, the idea that the central office would withhold funds from schools and decide what it would offer them makes little sense.

If schools did not get services from the central office, where would they turn? CMOs and talent suppliers like Teach For America and The New Teacher Project are available to provide teacher and principal preservice training. Vendors like Mass Insight, university-based providers, and support networks like the Coalition of Essential Schools are also supplying teacher in-service training, organizational assessment and development services, and school turnaround consulting.

In mature portfolio districts like New York, New Orleans, and Denver, assistance providers of the kinds described above are growing rapidly. Although those districts still have vestiges of the traditional central office, and the marketplace of independent providers is still not enough to meet all schools' needs, it is developing rapidly. Philanthropies are investing in vendor start-ups, via intermediaries like New Schools New Orleans.

Development of this support infrastructure is one of the most challenging but most promising elements of the governance change we propose. There will be fits, and starts, and continuous improvement in the marketplace, but these processes, over time, will result in improved service quality.

MAKE OR BUY: THE USE OF CONTRACTING IN A
REDESIGNED CENTRAL OFFICE

Just because central offices can decide something does not mean they have to provide it directly. There are a variety of reasons why many central office functions should be contracted out. Three considerations are important as districts decide whether to produce services directly or buy them from a vendor:

When a given function has a central governmental purpose, contracting does not usually make much sense. The cost of failure—from a poorly executed contract—is simply too high and would risk the buyer's reputation.

The costs associated with identifying suppliers as well as writing and monitoring contracts can reduce or eliminate any potential efficiency gains. Contracts are best used when several potential suppliers exist and when performance metrics are easily specified and monitored.

Some products or services benefit more from competitive market forces than others. For example, in the realm of curriculum products, diversity is so important that it might be worth employing multiple contractors even if a monopoly provider could operate more cheaply. Or, if existing approaches to professional development have proven to be inadequate or out-of-date, contracting could stimulate new provider creation and innovative approaches.

Table 6.1 overlays these considerations across aspects of district and school administration. It asks three questions: Is the function mission centric for the central office or schools? Are the costs for developing and monitoring the contract high? And would the function benefit from diversity or innovation? The answers to these three questions provide a scale (ranging from 0 to 3) to guide whether the functions should be developed and managed in-house or if contractors should be sought.

At one extreme are central office functions like compliance and portfolio management and school-level functions like hiring and budgeting in which few, if any, benefits emerge from contracting out. The central office (in the case of compliance and portfolio management) and the school (in the case of hiring and budgeting) should retain control of these functions by developing the expertise, systems, policies, and tools required to effectively

TABLE 6.1 Criteria for deciding whether to perform functions in the central office or by schools or to contract out

Function	Is it mission centric?	High or low transaction costs?	Benefit from diversity or innovation?	Make or buy?
Leadership	Yes	High	No	Make
Portfolio management	Yes	High	No	Make
Talent recruitment and management	No	Low	Yes	Buy
Data management	No	Low	No	Buy
Communications	No	Low	No	Buy
Enrollment	No	Low	No	Buy
Transportation	No	Low	No	Buy
Finance	Yes	High	No	Make
Professional development	No	Low	Yes	Buy
Hiring	Yes	High	No	Make
Budgeting	Yes	High	No	Make
Curriculum	Yes	Low	Yes	Buy
Academic supports	No	Low	Yes	Buy
Community supports	No	Low	Yes	Buy

manage them in-house. At the other end of the spectrum are things like talent recruitment, professional development, and community and academic supports in which there are few reasons to develop the functions internally and ample reasons to use contracting as a way to improve service quality.

In between these extremes is a range of functions in which there are some benefits to contracting but others to retaining the function in-house. For these, the decision to contract out will likely depend on the skill of the procurement office (low skill levels or inexperience may make these services more difficult to contract for), the market for providers (thin markets with few suppliers limit the benefits of contracting), and the demand for services (more varied demand will increase the benefits of contracting).

These attributes will also shape districts' longer-term strategies around the make or buy question and the use of contracting. For example, a thin market may make contracting out impractical in the short run. But the district might deploy strategies to lower barriers to entry for potential providers, thereby stimulating supply. This would be a smart strategy if contractors would be better suited to deliver the service in the long run owing to changing market demands.

TRANSITIONING TO A LEANER, MORE FOCUSED
CENTRAL OFFICE

With a strong logic for streamlining the central office while empowering schools as well as a strategy for utilizing contractors, it is worth considering *how* districts transform themselves into a leaner and more focused agency. It goes without saying that some of the changes discussed here are dependent on reforms made at other levels of government. Federal and state programs to target aid for particular students must be streamlined, consolidated, and integrated into a more cohesive school finance system (see chapter 7).

Even in the absence of change at higher levels of education governance, change in the central office is possible and will require careful coordination with schools. Most districts have a number of schools that are ready to function autonomously and take on some formerly district-provided functions. By devolving authority incrementally, the district can begin to shrink offices that it plans to eliminate entirely over the course of the transition. Alternatively, the district might spin off some functions to nonprofit providers. This has the dual benefit of maintaining continuity for schools that still require district assistance as well as stimulating the market for new providers where traditionally they are absent.

Other schools might need some time to prepare for autonomy by, for example, training the principal to handle hiring and budgets. These schools can become autonomous by the second or third year of the transition. Most districts will also have potential principals (teachers who are natural leaders but have not sought administrative certification, sharp assistant principals who would otherwise have to wait until retirements created principalship vacancies) who could with some support take over schools whose current leaders do not want or cannot handle autonomy. Districts might also use established charter management organizations to take over schools that lack capacity to self-govern or, alternatively, hire such organizations as consultants to support the transition to autonomy.

Conclusion

Transitioning to a leaner central office has two implications. One is that the central office will emerge as a more focused and coherent organization. A second is that it enables schools to control a much larger portion of education funding, resulting in more tailored supports for schools. Chapter 7 will discuss how school finance systems will evolve to support these transformations.

7

Allocation and Control of Public Funds

Governance and financing are not separable—a new system for one cannot operate as intended while leaving the other unchanged. There are two big problems with our current financing system. First, it tolerates a great deal of horizontal inequity, so that very different amounts can be spent on similar students in the same state and even the same district. This gives some schools big advantages over others and undermines any claim that schools can be fairly compared on performance.

Second, the system now does not provide real money to schools. It allocates money to district-wide programs, central office structures, administrative functions, a district-wide teaching force, a stock of buildings, and so forth. These are then distributed to schools via methods of the district's choosing; schools make do with the teachers and other resources they are given. This method of resource allocation does not allow the kinds of flexibility needed for innovation and competition. Money does not move from one school to another when a student transfers, and schools cannot make internal financial trade-offs, for example, spending less on teachers and facilities and more on online resources or student internships.

To support a diverse and innovative supply of schools, we must fund schools and students equitably, give schools a defined amount for every student who enrolls, and allow schools to set their own spending priorities. This chapter will show how these things can be done in the context of a constitutional governance system.

How We Got the Current System

The American approach to funding education, like its approach to governance, has emerged slowly and haphazardly, a product of politics and advocacy, not design. Starting in the 1950s as courts decided civil rights cases, Congress created new services and entitlement programs for particular groups. State legislatures started small programs to solve emergent problems, school employees sought job protections and control over their work assignments, universities sought gatekeeper status for potential teachers and administrators, and families sought advantages in the competition for the best school placements. The sum of these actions was the inflexible financing system we have today.

For example, the federal Elementary and Secondary Education Act included only a few programs when first enacted in 1965, but over time new funding streams and sets of regulations (for purposes as diverse as teacher professional development and bilingual education) proliferated. These processes led to a labyrinth of rules and regulations connected to an evergrowing network of separate funding paths, each with its own "allowable uses" and reporting requirements.

Under the current system, people with ideas about how to do things differently—to introduce some actions that cost money and to substitute them for other current uses of funds—have great difficulty getting their ideas adopted or even seriously tested. This limitation applies to incumbent teachers and principals in traditional public schools. Outsiders, observing that U.S. schools have remained about the same, despite revolutions in technology and economic life, conclude that education stasis is due to the lack of new ideas. But that is wrong. Individual teachers, principals, and technology innovators come up with new ideas about instruction all the time and often put them into small-scale practice as long as no one complains about it. But if a new practice generates imitators or publicity, it can be interpreted as something irregular and possibly threatening and be stopped.

Because funds cannot flow from established uses to new ones, good ideas cannot be fully developed or persuasively demonstrated. Imaginative people who have ideas about uses of technology will not expect that applications they invent for K–12 education can be funded, so they will likely apply themselves in other realms instead.

Today's funding arrangements for public education were not designed with innovation or continuous improvement in mind. They assume that a student will attend a specific school, in which teacher salaries and other costs are paid by the school district. School leaders get very little money to spend on their own because money flows to schools not in the form of cash but in the form of people and resources sent by the district. A school can lose one student (or in a typical district as many as nineteen) and not lose any resources. In the rare case in which a student might take some courses at another school or outside the district (e.g., at an alternative school for gifted children or at a community college) the district, not the school, pays extra costs out of a central fund. These threshold effects governing the use of resources can also undermine the intention to target funds toward particular groups of students, as in some localities schools below an arbitrary threshold (e.g., 35 percent low-income for the federal Title I program) receive no assistance.

Our system is built to support schools that students attend all day every day and whose employees provide all the instruction a child needs to gain credit for a year's learning. It is more difficult to get public funds to blended or hybrid schools that provide some instruction via computer online and some via in-person teaching. Even if states and school districts permit money to flow to virtual schools, the funding status of blended schools would be precarious. States and districts could decide that blended schools were attracting too many students and drawing too much money out of their conventional schools and revoke policies that let funds flow to them.

How a Constitutional Governance System Would Fund Education

What would transparent and fair school finance system look like? It would need to

- fund education not institutions,
- move money as students move,
- pay for unconventional forms of instruction,
- pay for facilities without privileging conventional school models,
- withhold funding for ineffective programs without chilling innovation, and
- adapt funding levels and weights in light of experience.

FUNDING EDUCATION NOT INSTITUTIONS

How can states and local CECs provide money for K–12 education in ways that allow continuous improvement?[1] The answer is that states and localities should fund something that is permanent, not contingent, and tie money to the one element of the education system to which they are unconditionally committed—students.

This means designating a specific amount for every child in the state and distributing money to districts and schools solely on the basis of enrollment. Under a constitutional governance system, the state could opt to "weight" pupil-based funding by allocating more for one group of children than for another (e.g., providing more than the average amount of money to support the education of disabled or English language learners or those in high-risk communities).

States might let spending vary owing to variations in local taxable assets and tax effort. If local spending differences were correlated with local costs (e.g., low spending only in low-wage and low property value areas), this would not undermine the "level playing field" principle. However, if some localities (e.g., large urban districts) ended up spending less despite high local costs, children in those schools would get less. Moreover, families' abilities to enroll children in schools run by better funded districts would be limited by the fact that those children would bring less money than other children those districts might enroll. Thus, children in poorly funded districts would have fewer opportunities, and the schools in those localities would, ironically, experience less competition than schools in better funded localities.

The principles of a level playing field and funding students not institutions lead to the conclusion that the state should fund education uniformly, meaning that a child with certain characteristics would get the same amount of money no matter where in the state she lives.

The CEC, state, and federal governments would not mandate particular uses of funds or support particular programs, administrative structures, or salary scales. Of course, there would be some constraints on the use of funds—to support only schools that subjected themselves to CEC oversight and agreed to participate in the local enrollment system that ensures fair and equitable access to schools.

Districts could skim off very little money, and that would be used for central functions like data collection and analysis, administration of enrollment lottery systems, and decisions about what schools to open or close. The CEC would not be able to tax schools for services that other entities were also capable of providing (see chapter 6). The CEC, central office employees, and school leaders would all know exactly how much the central office spends and for what and understand that every dollar spent at the district level cannot be used by schools to educate students. Thus, all parties would have incentives to minimize and justify any district-level spending.

If states and localities would combine all the money they now spend on K–12 education and divide it up by enrollment, with the same or weighted fraction of the total assigned to each child, and distribute dollars to schools in the same way, they could simultaneously eliminate the barriers to innovation and to improvement that are inherent in current funding systems. In a constitutional governance system where central administrative costs are very low, most schools would also get dramatically more money than they receive now. This would allow new uses of funds, an essential precondition to innovation.

Consistent with the discussion of the federal role in chapter 4, the federal government could reinforce the movement toward pupil-based funding by making its major grant programs pupil specific. It could do that by sharply defining student eligibility criteria for such programs as Title I and IDEA, then requiring that states divide the money received from any such program equitably among all eligible recipients in the state, and allocating it as extra money to the schools those children attend. Thus, federal programs could still increase spending on designated beneficiaries without privileging particular uses. Although there would still be some costs associated with counting eligible beneficiaries and distributing dollars to districts, this arrangement would greatly cut the share of federal funds used to ensure that funds are used only in specified ways, and in ways that cannot inadvertently benefit noneligible students.[2]

MOVE MONEY AS STUDENTS MOVE

Funding students (and not programs) is a step in the right direction, but it is not enough. States must also make sure that all funds move from one district, school, or instruction provider to another as students transfer. Schools that lose students should lose the income associated with them in some defined period, say, by the end of the current semester, and schools gaining students should get the extra money as soon as it is taken from the school of origin. This makes family choice significant for everyone: students could move whenever their parents identified a more suitable school or set of instructional programs or as ineffective schools were closed and students shifted to more effective ones.

Charter school funding establishes a rudimentary version

of such a system. Funds follow students directly to the charter schools they attend and are taken away from schools that pupils transfer away from.

State charter laws are imperfect in many ways, including the fact that they only apply to students who transfer to such schools; all other students are still in district-provided schools where funds are tied up, hidden, and inflexible. Many states, moreover, leave some funding behind in district-run public schools even when pupils transfer to charter schools. Depending on state and charter laws and local policies, charter students either do or do not benefit from public funds allocated for federal programs, transportation, and facilities. Charter students often do not benefit from locally raised funds (e.g., from property tax levies).

However, the basic charter paradigm is a good frame for the funding mechanism to be attached to a constitutional governance scheme. Chartering ensures funding based on enrollment and school freedom over spending, staffing, and use of time. A funding system would have to apply to all students no matter what publicly funded school they attended. As with chartering, the school a student attended—whether it provided all the students' courses or purchased some from other sources—would be accountable for results: test scores, credits, ability to take more advanced courses, and ultimately graduation and college eligibility.

Funds available for a child's education must include all the taxpayer funds available to support a student's education. To make this happen, some government entity, likely the local district central office, would need to assemble all of the funds available from all sources for K–12 education in a locality, keep an account for every student, and faithfully allocate its contents to whatever school or education program a student attends.

A new kind of public entity, possibly a county or regional finance office of the state government, could be an alternative. It could assemble and disburse all funds. It would also account for funds on a pupil basis. Every student would have an account that showed what funding from all sources was available for his education and to what schools and vendors it had been disbursed.

Each student's account would, in a sense, constitute a backpack of funding that the student would carry with her to any eligible school in which she enrolls. The contents of the backpack would be flexible dollars, not coupons whose use is restricted to a particular course or service.

Under a constitutional governance scheme, no school enrolling backpack-wearing students could charge tuition in excess of the full amount in a student's backpack. Schools and other providers could also offer partial instructional programs, and students and their families could mix and match to the limit of the funds in the backpack. (See below for possible safeguards against misuse of backpack funds.)

Backpack-based movement of funds with students would impact existing schools' budgets promptly, creating incentives for schools to avoid losing students to other schools. Innovators (educators and social service professionals with new ideas) would also be encouraged by the certainty that they could get full funding for every student enrolled in their school or program.

ALLOW SCHOOLS TO PAY FOR UNCONVENTIONAL FORMS OF INSTRUCTION

For free movement of funds to promote experimentation and innovation, it must be possible for students to enroll in schools that are configured in novel ways. Technology opens up the possibility of students learning in a one-to-one relationship with a computer-based system, or linking to a set of lectures and other presentation materials along with literally thousands of other students, or receiving their instruction through a mix of technology- and teacher-delivered approaches. These approaches are not certain to work in every case, but the system must be designed to allow such differentiation and track results closely.

Schools could pursue very different strategies—some spending all their money on teachers and a conventional building, others purchasing some instruction from other schools or online, and others serving only as brokers—assessing the effectiveness of various instructional providers and assigning individual students to the ones most likely to meet their needs. Students would be able to join online courses provided by schools other than the one they normally attend and could take advantage of courses that combine experiential learning (e.g., participation in workplaces, arts events, or social services) with online materials that prepare students for those experiences and assess learning.

Such "broker" schools would buy most of the instruction their students receive from others: their contribution, and the justification for their keeping some of the funds that come in the backpack, would be identification of the best matches for an individual student. Schools that did this well would prosper, but those that did it poorly would fail quickly and disappear.

This would create strong incentives for local CECs to search for the best way to meet any student's need and to be indifferent about whether a student takes a course delivered by his neighborhood school or some other source. Most schools will continue to offer adult supervision, counseling, and tutoring, and some will develop instructional specialties that both keep their students at home and draw students enrolled elsewhere. But to be competitive, especially under an accountability system that takes account of productivity, schools will need to organize themselves for nimbleness, directly delivering only those courses and other aspects of the student experience at which they are good and "buying" others from other schools or vendors. Thus, a school might employ teachers in English and the arts and buy physics and math instruction and extracurricular experiences like outdoor leadership and advanced sports instruction from others. In effect, schools will constitute a marketplace for instructional programs and other services, each trying to be an excellent provider (and thus seller) of some things and a buyer of others.

BUNDLE FACILITIES FUNDING INTO THE
STUDENT BACKPACK

Schools and instruction providers should not be punished for being efficient. Blended schools might save money on teachers and/or facilities. Virtual and broker schools could, if they attract enough students, pay far less to educate each additional student than they receive from student backpacks. These results are desirable because they can support investment. Even if providers are nonprofits, the low marginal costs of online instruction can enable continual investment in new and improved resources.

To create a fully level playing field for competition among all schools, states would need to add the funds now set aside for facilities construction and maintenance to the student backpack. States now fund separate line items for construction and building maintenance, and these are not counted in calculations of school operating costs. Thus, even if online schools were equitably funded on school operating costs, traditional schools would get a significant extra subsidy.

In a time when innovation is necessary, and the cost structures of different forms of schooling will differ dramatically, a special subsidy for bricks and mortar is counterproductive. It defrays cost borne by one kind of school, while ignoring the investment costs of online schools, which must pay for computers, methods development, and back-office administration out of their operating costs.

Under this arrangement, a school—whether traditional, hybrid, or online—would pay whatever facilities costs it used. Schools and instructional program providers with high equipment, research and development, and oversight costs could pay these from funds recovered from student backpacks, just as schools paying high rents could meet those costs. In the long run, this arrangement would probably lead conventional schools to reduce their costs by renting less space and refusing to pay for expensive amenities like theaters and swimming pools.

This neat solution might not work perfectly in cities where facilities costs vary sharply from one neighborhood to another (e.g., from a dense downtown area to a changing area with high vacancy rates). In such cases local CECs might need to add a weight related to a student's neighborhood of residence to the backpack. These students would then become even more attractive to schools that had figured out how to minimize their facilities costs.

WITHHOLD FUNDING FOR INEFFECTIVE SCHOOLS

A funding system that is open to innovation must also have a mechanism for deciding which schools and instructional programs should be considered eligible to enroll students. A financing system must include arrangements to withhold or withdraw funds from ineffective providers.

For whole schools, including hybrid and virtual schools, chartering provides a useable framework for performance management. The CEC as a charter authorizer can close low performing charter schools or refuse to renew their authorization. Hybrid and virtual schools can be evaluated on the same standards, tests, and other measures of student progress as those used for conventional schools, and charters for low performers can be cancelled or not renewed.

Oversight of hybrid and virtual schools is a new demand that traditional local school boards are not organized to meet. CECs would be better designed for this function because they would not operate any schools or own any facilities and therefore not care what a school's cost structure was, as long as it was effective.

MAXIMIZE PARENTS' OPTIONS WITHOUT LOSING SCHOOL ACCOUNTABILITY

Even if parents chose the schools their children attended, the options available to students, and the opportunities for entrepreneurs, are still limited by the imaginations and tastes of current school operators. Of course, parents could be given full access to their children's backpacks and allowed to purchase any combination of instructional experiences they wanted from any source. What children learn would then depend on the quality of their parents' choices.

In the long run parents might learn to do this well, and the supply of good options could rise to meet the demand. However, students or parents could make bad purchases, so that students did not learn what they needed to graduate or succeed in higher education and work. In those situations, would the children simply be out of luck? Could the parents be punished in some way that was not counterproductive for all involved? Or would the public be forced to pay again for instruction the student should have gotten the first time?

As the senior author has argued elsewhere, giving parents unlimited control of the student's backpack could fatally compromise performance accountability.[3] However, there are two ways that parents could have important choices, while maintaining the principle that one entity, the school, is responsible for a student's overall learning:

1. limiting the amount of money parents can dispose of; and
2. limiting parents' choices to supplementary or enrichment programs.

Parents could be required to choose a whole school provider, but each provider could set aside a limited amount from each student's backpack that could be used to pay for tutoring and enrichment programs. Schools could offer cafeteria plans[4] for extracurricular activities and supplementary learning (either online or in person). Students and families would then be free to shop for the best combination of courses and experiences their set-aside funds could cover.

Parents could control this limited amount, choosing the enrichment but not the core instructional programs. This would both increase families' control over children's educational experience and allow some public funds to flow to new and innovative programs. Providers of enrichment and support programs could receive some public funds, yet families could not be led into making choices that compromised their children's core instruction. Providers would face competition, both on the quality and effectiveness of their services and on cost.

Schools could even compete on the quality of their cafeteria plans and on the amounts of money available for families to control. Although schools that put too much money under families' control might risk failure if their students then could not meet key performance standards, schools would have a strong incentive to let families control something important and help families choose effective programs.

This arrangement would eliminate the need for the CEC to vet every online provider or to negotiate with vendors about costs. Costs of supplementary services would be regulated by the amounts schools decide to make available, and parents would have incentives to avoid vendors that required all of their available funds for one service.[5]

ADAPT FUNDING IN LIGHT OF EXPERIENCE

Understanding that what works best for one group of children might not be so for other groups (e.g., well-supported native-born middle-class children versus immigrants from war-torn countries who missed some years of school), the constitutional governance system would try to link spending levels to student characteristics. It would then employ a weighted student funding system whose weights would be determined by the estimated cost of delivering services to a given group of children.

Any resemblance between this approach to determining spending levels and the "adequacy" arguments made by some to escalate spending on U.S. schools is illusory.[6] Spending levels would be based on the most efficient, not the average or the most expensive, approach to meeting the needs of a given group of children.

Weights for particular groups would be set according to demonstrated performance, not (as in the case of adequacy arguments) according to simulations of what programs of unknown character might achieve. Thus, weighting would be conservative. Today, weights for disadvantaged children could be based on the full cost of delivering simple but highly focused and disciplined instructional programs, resembling traditional Catholic parochial schools or newer "no excuses" models like KIPP, the Knowledge is Power Program, a network of middle and high schools designed to meet the needs of disadvantaged minority youth.

The constitutional governance system would encourage trials of new approaches, especially for the education of children whom no existing set of schools serves well. If and when new approaches, for example, combinations of in-person and computer-based instruction with specific ancillary supports, prove uniquely productive for a particular group of students, the governance and financing system needs to adapt to the evidence. That can mean increasing spending for particular groups of students, at least until something equally effective and less expensive comes along.

Conclusion

A funding system cannot cause innovation or equity: it can only encourage it, or interfere. Whether innovation occurs, at what pace, and to what ultimate benefit depend on factors other than public funding. But a system like the one described here would make promising breakthroughs much more likely to scale rapidly. Likewise, no funding system can guarantee equitable opportunities or outcomes for children coming from different backgrounds, but it can certainly make them more likely. The next chapter describes the path toward enacting the system we have described into law and the likely challenges along the way.

8

Enacting the System into Law and Managing Implementation Politics

We have called the new governance system constitutional because it limits the authority of elected officials and creates checks and balances between policy-making bodies and concerned interests. However, it will not necessarily become part of any state's written constitution. Instead, it will be based on state statute, enacted by the legislature and signed by the governor. It will also be implemented by people and organizations that have their own priorities, not all of which will be aligned with the principles of constitutional governance. Thus, no matter how clearly the new governance system is defined, its emergence and long-term functioning will rely on things that cannot be created by the black letters of law—discipline, diligence, and political organization.

This chapter asks two questions: What will have to happen in order for such a profound change in state and local powers and functions to be enacted into law? And, once such a law is enacted, what is to prevent problems that can arise over time via lax implementation and political pressure?

The (Long, Bumpy) Road to New Governance

Policy change is never easy. The current system of laws, regulations, contracts, and institutional roles is deeply defended by political organization. Groups representing unions, school administrators, school boards, and parents are well organized, and state legislative committees and departments of education reflect this mobilization.

State legislators and governors are not always well positioned to overcome these forces. As Terry Moe has shown, the Democratic Party benefits from the support of teachers unions in the form of money and manpower, a fact that can make support for reform equivalent to political suicide for some officeholders.[1] The end result is that many representatives are committed to the preservation of specific institutions and mandates, not to advancing the performance of local school systems.

If the old system is defended to such a degree, can it be changed? We believe the answer is yes, but probably not cut from whole cloth. Instead, it is being formed a piece at a time, like a quilt, with some reforms, such as pupil-based school finance systems, setting the stage for others, like universal parental choice.

Some movement toward a constitutional system has already started. In many big-city school systems, via special state emergency legislation, mayors and district superintendents are bypassing political, regulatory, and contractual constraints.[2] Special state laws now define K–12 governance in New Orleans, New York City, Detroit, Los Angeles, and Cleveland.[3] The laws enacted to date are not rigorously "constitutional" in the sense defined above. However, the principles embedded in such laws— performance-based accountability for schools, pupil-based funding, family choice, openness to new school providers and teachers—are movements toward the system outlined in the previous chapters and will set precedents that can be applied more readily to other districts.

On a small scale, the movement toward constitutional governance has also spread to a few state education agencies, caused both by the need to accommodate the governance reforms being

BOX 8.1 The Cleveland Plan

In 2012, Cleveland mayor Frank Jackson updated and expanded upon the 2010 district transformation plan with a focus on expanding the number of high-performing district and charter schools in the city, as well as working with state legislators to remove barriers to full implementation of the plan. As a result of the mayor's advocacy as well as the support of several local foundations, the Ohio General Assembly passed legislation that enabled greater school autonomy and established incentives for districts and charters to partner. The key provisions include greater flexibility for principals around staffing, budgets, and school calendars, as well as an innovative provision that would share some local levy dollars with participating charters.

advanced in cities and by governors and state superintendents who want to remission their agencies to emphasize performance improvement.[4]

Governance change is also spreading to smaller cities. In Louisiana, Jefferson Parish, Baton Rouge, Lafayette, and Shreveport have joined New Orleans to implement governance reform. At least part of a special law enacted for Cleveland in early 2012 is likely to be applied to Columbus and other cities. The principles of New York City's mayoral control statute are being applied statewide via the state's Race to the Top grant.

To date, these special laws and their application in an increasing number of districts have not been as systematic and logically complete as the governance scheme described in this book. For these ideas to be broadly enacted, advocates will need to find ways to break out of the confines of specialized institutions like education committees in state legislatures and school boards, who are too beholden to entrenched interests to support significant changes to the status quo. As Jeffrey Henig shows, this is already happening—educational governance is becoming less isolated and more open to initiatives from leaders of general government.[5]

However, to build momentum around these reforms, advocacy groups will have to adopt reform as a long-term goal. Long-term advocacy of a package of legislative changes for education is not unprecedented. An early example of fifty-state adoption of a new policy framework is provided by the National Business Roundtable's push for standards-based reform in the early 1990s. The Roundtable endorsed a common policy framework and organized state-based CEOs and their lobbying organizations in all fifty states to work for its adoption. The result was a rapid adoption of key ideas that drove education reform through the 1990s. It petered out only when the limitations of the reform strategy, which worked around rather than through the existing governance system, became apparent.

More recently, the push for Common Core State Standards, led by the National Governors Association, the Council of Chief State School Officers, and state-based advocacy groups (e.g., Tennessee SCORE), provides another example of a broad-based coalition of groups pushing for reforms. In the case of the Common Core, the initiative spread further and faster but also drew more opposition due to federal efforts to incentivize adoption. A similar approach, with less overt federal pressure, could promote widespread adoption of constitutional governance.

Leaders at the state level could advance governance reform by setting in place rules by which existing districts are integrated into the new system. Many states already have the power to seize control of districts that fail to meet academic targets or are in financial failure. Integrating these districts into the governance scheme first would enable a more incremental approach to putting the system into place. But failure is not the only path. Some districts, eager for greater freedom from state mandates and regulation and more control over resources, might opt into the system, either by popular vote or via the local school board.

Of course, there is nothing inevitable about this. The localities now using key elements of a constitutional governance system have to experience some benefits, and implementation must be managed carefully. At present the results—in cities as diverse as New Orleans, New York City, Denver, Baltimore, and Hartford, are positive enough to sustain local reform efforts and to spread to other cities, although their permanency is far from guaranteed.[6] State leaders, especially those affiliated with Chiefs for Change—are pursuing complementary changes in state legal frameworks and agency structure.

We do not think the movement to constitutional governance will be rapid. Some aspects of the system will spread faster and further than others, depending on their implementation costs and political popularity. Others are likely to be adopted first in states with major metropolitan areas and within those states applied to larger localities earlier than to smaller ones. It might not be possible, for example, for smaller rural school boards to make the transition from directly operating schools to overseeing independent providers until a significant supply of school providers have developed in metropolitan, suburban, and large town jurisdictions.

Managing the Inevitable Political Pressures

Critics of the ideas presented here would not be doing their jobs if they did not point out—as the authors have written many times before—that our current governance system emerged as a result of many incremental, often well-intentioned, accommodations. Even if adoption of a constitutional governance system gave public education a fresh start, wouldn't it eventually end up looking pretty much as it does now?

Our political system is designed to accommodate organized groups, each of which pursues its own interests by continually pressing for what look like small changes in policy. General interests often suffer in these arrangements because they are poorly organized and weakly attentive to how these small changes affect them. The history of school reform suggests groups will push for

- special privileges or favors for some school providers,
- lax accountability that allows schools to continue operating despite low performance,
- rules that exclude certain groups of children from testing, and
- bureaucratic controls and prescriptive mandates that erode school autonomy.[7]

Managing these inevitable pressures for policy evolution are central to governing. While erosion of reform strategies is always a possibility, many reforms survive virtually intact because reform leaders and advocates actively resist efforts by opponents from the outset. Moreover, policy feedback—the remodeling of the interest group environment as supporters are strengthened by the flow of public funds and benefits, while groups that depended on an earlier regime are weakened—can stabilize a reform.[8]

Preventing Provider Capture

The mobilization of new groups can stabilize, but also possibly corrupt, the new governance. New organizations that provide government-funded services try to maximize the benefits they gain (by excluding others) and to bias governmental decision making in their favor (by developing close relationships with government officials). These two possibilities are both evident in the State of Ohio, where the first online instruction vendors sponsored by the state are working hard to prevent competitors from getting a foothold in the market and for-profit charter providers have campaigned successfully for legislative language that lets them avoid demanding public oversight.

Concerns about provider capture are serious in any reform that requires government to contract for rather than directly deliver a service. Unlike private sector contracting, where purchasers have strong incentives to avoid being dominated by the firms they hire, government officials know that contractors are constituents as well as vendors. Contractors have strong incentives to contribute to the campaigns of key officials and even to encourage friendly parties to run for office. Teachers unions, the main K–12 contractor under traditional governance, built disproportionate influence this way. Analogous developments will occur under the new governance unless they are headed off.

While the constitutional framework attempts to check political impulses via rules and institutional design, interest groups will work to alter this basic framework to gain advantage. In order to counter the inherent advantage held by provider groups, leaders of reform must be proactive in organizing other concerned interests. Parents, community organizations, philanthropies, and businesses all have a stake in the education system and would be harmed by provider capture. However, they rarely engage in the kind of sustained and active engagement that is required to check other groups' influence. But when such groups do pay attention, they can be very effective at holding elected officials accountable for their policy decisions.[9]

One potential local counterforce against provider capture is sustained "civic oversight," provided by a high-level coalition whose purpose is to make sure that the city's general interest in effective schooling trumps' providers' commercial interests. Although in theory the CEC should serve this function, its susceptibility to capture suggests the need for an additional backstop. As the current authors have described elsewhere, a civic coalition, led by former mayors, leaders of businesses, religious leaders, and foundation heads, can perform this function.[10] The civic coalition can publish independent assessments of school performance and equity, update the list of problems needing solutions, recruit individuals who are not beholden to providers to fill seats on the CEC, and press to make sure that searches for new district CEOs are done in light of a long-range school improvement strategy. A civic coalition would be nongovernmental; it would essentially be an interest group with enough muscle to sustain support for strong public oversight and resist vendor monopolies.

In addition to monitoring the CEC, the civic oversight group could help support a diverse provider marketplace by providing start-up funding to groups with promising school models. Each of these functions help to inform the CEC as well as check the claims of other interests, including provider groups.

Managing the Pressure to Backslide on Oversight

Maintaining the search for continuous improvement is difficult because schools are community institutions designed to serve many purposes. A failing school may still be the pride of the neighborhood. Attaching negative labels to it, or worse yet, attempting to close its doors, is guaranteed to stir opposition from those who value it. Their concerns are not simply the result of misinformation. School closures inevitably impose short-term costs on a group of people in an effort to improve the "greater good."

As the checks and balances section of chapter 4 explains, CECs will experience pressures from the state to find alternatives for children in unproductive schools. The state can take away struggling schools that CECs will not close or change providers and put them under the control of a statewide school district. The state can also dismiss a CEC, order new elections, or assign its responsibilities to another CEC. The local schools' CEO can petition the state for help if the CEC consistently rejects her proposals to close or reassign management of a school.

There are also purely local measures that would help a CEC take bold action when needed. CECs themselves can reduce the zero-sum nature of a school closure decision by making it clear what options will be available for students before a closure decision is announced. It can also reassure neighbors that a school will still operate in their area—but under new management and with a better defined instructional program. School districts have more than once bungled the implementation of oversight systems—closing the doors of schools without considering whether families have any better options available to them.[11] School closures that result in children attending lower quality schools have measurable costs in terms of student achievement, but when those same children move to a higher performing school, measurable gains are possible.[12]

Oversight decisions are never simple, and schools cannot be evaluated on their own merits but must also be evaluated in terms of the other options available. Oversight bodies can and should make different decisions about two schools with equivalent achievement profiles but with different alternatives available to families.

When financially possible, CECs might also open new schools in ill-served areas and let them compete with existing schools, without forcing any immediate closures. Using parental choice to drive the process of winding down poorly performing schools makes the issue less political. In some cases, the leaders of weak schools that have lost out in competition for students have made their own closure decisions.[13] This can reduce the impression that a school closure is done to, rather than for, the neighborhood.

Managing the pace of school closures and provider changes is essential to sustaining reform. It is tempting to push reform as far and as fast as possible, limit engagement with the opposition, and be uncompromising in the pursuit of rapid change. But acting quickly and decisively can leave key supporters behind and put the whole enterprise on shaky ground. This was a key challenge in New York, where ambitious reforms faced an uncertain future when their chief champion—Mayor Michael Bloomberg—stepped down.

The CEC and CEO must make engagement and communication a centerpiece of the oversight system. Managing this is not just about trumpeting successes, although this is important. Districts leaders must expose reforms to scrutiny and acknowledge mistakes; otherwise opponents will do so.

Ensuring Fair Access and Treatment for All Students

Ensuring fair access and treatment of different students in public education is a perennial problem. Individuals and groups will always seek to create privileges, special opportunities, and disproportionate funding for themselves and their allies. The ways this happens varies. In a traditional system where the most consequential decisions are made by an elected school board or a complex bureaucracy, groups will focus on getting all they can through board elections and by controlling bureaucratic decisions. In a constitutional system where decisions about student placement, school spending, or employment are made at the school level, that is where self-seeking efforts will focus.

As the senior author has shown elsewhere, self-seeking occurs under all forms of governance; what varies is where it occurs and whether it is easy or difficult to observe.[14] Choice-based systems are open to self-seeking by schools, which have incentives to manipulate the admissions and expulsions process to get an easier-to-educate clientele, and by parents, who want their children to gain admissions advantages.

Any attempt to reform public education must deal with these thorny issues. Cities' and states' ongoing experiments with charter schools, vouchers, and other forms of choice suggest that not enough is being done to ensure that all children have access to high-quality options.

Legislation establishing constitutional governance must unambiguously establish the principles of equitable student access, funding, and fair competition among providers. It should also require procedures that have proven necessary in districts operating with multiple providers, including common admissions lotteries (which prevent schools from rigging the timing or design of their lotteries to get the students they most want); an annual review of student admissions, expulsion, and performance; and published procedures and criteria for selection of school providers and school closing.

Civil rights protections guarantee that discrimination against students in protected classes will land schools in court. Court-made rules could destabilize the governance system. Leaders must be proactive in both design and monitoring of oversight institutions to ensure that schools do not have the option of excluding hard-to-educate kids.

These provisions will allow civic-minded people to monitor results and identify inequities in practice. But they will not work unless aggressively used. The civic oversight group described above could promote equity throughout the system by monitoring and reporting on the fairness of student admissions and expulsions throughout the city—both processes and outcomes. Some localities have also protected children whose parents are negligent about expressing school preferences by appointing special-purpose guardians to fill out choice forms. Perhaps most importantly, New Orleans has created a citywide special education collaborative, under which schools pool funds to pay for extraordinarily expensive special education placements and create reciprocal service agreements so that a student admitted to any school can get the best services available in the city.

These ideas are a place to start. City leaders who are serious about governance reform will not wait until discrimination or scandal has arisen. They will monitor results closely knowing that self-seeking will occur and that it will be come widespread unless exposed and blocked.

Resisting Bureaucratization

The final threat to constitutional governance is the fact that policy makers generally solve problems by creating new policies and administrative structures. These habits are strong because they allow public officials to claim that they have solved a problem when all they have done is written a rule or made a delegation. While such efforts are often well intentioned, the results can undermine school autonomy and problem solving.

Under constitutional governance, problems will arise, and the pressure for rule making will be strong and sometimes irresistible. If one school cheats on admissions or expels a student arbitrarily, someone—the local CEC, CEO, or the state—will be tempted to write a new policy. The same will be true when aspiring school vendors ask when they will get a chance to compete for a charter or contract and want to know exactly what they must do to win. New rules can look like sensible responses to a problem. But remembering that the overregulation affecting schools under traditional K–12 governance accumulated one rule at a time, officials responsible for constitutional governance must be alert to the dangers of incrementalism.

The school bill of rights and other principles explained in chapter 5 will make it easier for public officials to manage cases without new policies or regulation. But they will encounter re-

lentless pressures to issue directives, guidelines, letters of clarifi-
cation, and other instruments. As described in chapter 5, school
providers and their associations will have to be vigilant about
identifying such instruments that violate the bill of rights and
appeal to the state and ultimately the courts.

Changing State Legislatures

Of course, regulation and bureaucratization can also come from
the state level. The basic framing statutes for constitutional governance can be thrown out or eroded by actions of future legislative majorities. Future legislatures might forget why constitutional governance was created in the first place. Some legislators
might want to build their legislative records by proposing new
categorical programs that would constrain all schools. Others
might propose changes at the behest of interest groups, for example, teachers unions that would like to go back to the days
when they could negotiate a single collective bargaining agreement for a whole district.

Nothing can absolutely prevent legislators from proposing
changes that would erode constitutional governance. But, in addition to bringing in new interests that have a stake in maintaining reform, reform leaders may consider pressing state legislative
leaders to build barriers to change into the legislative process.

Changing the legislative process can be done in two ways.
First, increasing the number of actors who must agree renders
policy change more difficult. The statute setting up the constitutional governance system could be written in such a way that
amendments could be made only by a supermajority of legislators. Such requirements are not unprecedented. The challenge
in using this approach is that closely divided state legislatures,
where leaders must work hard to assemble a narrow majority just
to pass initial reform, are unlikely to agree to institute rules that
will be extremely difficult to change.

A second strategy relies on changes to committee structures in state legislatures. In most states, the organization of state legislative committees mirrors our current governance system. Most legislators choose to work on subjects that interest them, so legislative committees on education become magnets for activists related to different education "causes." In education, as in other fields, current legislative committee structure promotes narrowly defined interests at the expense of more diffuse, general interests.

State legislative leaders (i.e., the speaker and senate president) could create more broadly based work on education by making education a subcommittee of appropriations so it would become interesting to people concerned more with productivity than with details of educational practice. Alternatively, legislative leaders could keep education-focused committees but forbid the formation of any subcommittees, thus diluting the influence of single-issue members or those linked to particular interests. Finally, legislative leaders could require all proposals for new state programs to be independently analyzed with respect to their implications for innovation and school freedom of action.

These actions could not be written into law, so they would need to be constantly defended and renewed. By themselves, they could not prevent erosion of constitutional governance. But they could be effective if done in combination with the other political and institutional changes suggested above.

Conclusion

Adoption of constitutional governance for public education could insulate schools from some forms of politics that have crippled districts and schools. But governance change is political action, and there is no sure way to rule out opposing political action that would weaken schools, bias competition, and protect incumbents. Sustainable reform depends on both strong policy design and careful implementation. Multiple, nested oversight structures and transparent fiscal and oversight standards make provider capture more difficult, facilitate stronger public support for reform, and protect against bureaucratic encroachment. But even with these design elements, implementation must be managed with an eye toward organizing natural allies and avoiding actions that unnecessarily alienate potential beneficiaries. The final chapter suggests how states and localities could make the transition from the current governance system to a constitutional one.

9

What Governance Change Can and Cannot Accomplish

This book began with the assertion that the current governance of K–12 public education limits its effectiveness and ability to improve. Our current governance system was created to provide good schools but has incrementally and inexorably changed to one that serves the interests of the most demanding adults and neglects the needs of many children. We have presented an alternative governance system that should be more focused on the needs of children and open to change, effective problem solving, and innovation.

We have described how a constitutional governance system will work and what kinds of laws, funding programs, and institutions it will require. These changes are moves in the right direction, but they are not sufficient in themselves to change the quality of education children receive. Children learn in schools and from teachers, not from governance systems.

The results of governance change will depend on whether schools are able to focus instruction on the needs of the particular children they serve, give children opportunities to learn high-level information and skills, and do so in a way that motivates student effort. By giving schools freedom about hiring and uses of time and money, and providing natural consequences for high and low performance, the constitutional governance system creates conditions that allow these things to happen. These conditions can also

- break down barriers that have limited jobs in education to an arbitrarily defined subset of all the educated adults in community,
- attract into K–12 education capable adults with a broader range of skills than now lead and teach in K–12 schools, and
- encourage innovators with new ideas about uses of technology as support for student and teacher work.

Will localities that adopt constitutional governance realize all these potential benefits? Everything depends on how communities perceive the opportunities given them.

When a state enacts the laws necessary to create a constitutional governance system, the majority of schools will be still run by the district and depend on the central office for direction and services. Virtually all teachers will be hired and employed by the district, not by individual schools, and be covered by the districtwide collective bargaining agreement. How will the transition between the current realities and the new system in full operation be made? It would entail

- conversion of schools from district-run to self-managing status;
- major reallocations of funds on the basis of student enrollment;
- completely new roles for school district CEOs, as managers of a slate of autonomous but accountable schools;
- new, sharply defined roles for a much smaller central office;
- changes in who teaches and how teachers are employed;
- a new market system for providing school improvement services; and
- a much stronger role for parents.

How Localities Can Make the Transition

Newly empowered CECs will need to make the implied changes—shrinking their central offices to a tiny fraction of their current size, putting all of the money into student backpack accounts, making existing schools into autonomous charter-like organizations, transferring teachers from district to school payrolls, identifying providers for needed new schools, and closing the least effective current ones—over a few years.

The transformation stage will require investments in training and capacity building at the district and school levels. These training costs might be met by reductions in central office spending. However, special state and philanthropic transition funds could allow district leaders to transfer funds from the central office to schools immediately.

The district CEO should be in charge of transition, via a plan approved annually by the new CEC. Key actions in the transition to a new constitutional governance scheme would include the following:

- Adopting a performance rating plan for schools.
- Setting criteria for transforming or replacing the lowest performing schools in the cities by establishing new autonomous leadership teams or chartering to an independent provider.
- Establishing a unit whose job is to develop or new leadership or charter operators for school replacements.
- Evaluating existing central office roles, hiring for expertise to perform new governance functions, and shrinking remaining central office staff.
- In conjunction with shrinking the central office, proportionately increasing the amounts of funding controlled directly by schools and allowing schools to purchase services—teacher professional development, technical advice, and accounting and legal services.
- Giving existing central office units that provide services to schools one year and a small budget to create a business plan for becoming independent legal entities to be supported by voluntary fees paid by autonomous schools.
- Stopping the hiring of teachers at the district level immediately and starting the collection of data on teacher applications from which schools can find teachers—whether from among incumbents or newcomers.
- Offering one year of district-funded training for incumbent school leaders to help take their schools into autonomous status.

- Starting the production of school report cards and other information packets to inform parents about all the choices available to them.
- Moving within two years to let all parents choose schools outside their neighborhoods if they wish and moving to a universal choice system and centrally administered lottery within five years.
- Transferring roughly one-fifth of their existing schools into a new autonomous/performance-based status annually for five years. During the transition, some schools will be ready for full autonomy and budget control earlier than others. This involves legally terminating the existing district school, helping school leaders form a legal entity that can receive funds, hire staff, and fulfill a performance contract, and starting the school again as an independent organization.
- Transferring teachers to school-based employment as soon as the schools become autonomous. Phasing out the district-wide teacher collective bargaining agreement gradually until all teachers work for schools, not the district.
- After five years, permanently closing all remaining district-run schools that are not ready to transfer into autonomous status and replacing them with new independently run charter schools.

Some Cities Are on the Way

A number of major cities are already moving in these directions. We have written previously[1] about cities, now more than twenty-five in number, that have adopted the portfolio strategy.[2] The Portfolio District Network, a national support organization for conventional school districts in transition, has identified seven foci of change: good options and choice for all families, school autonomy, pupil-based funding for all schools, talent seeking, independent sources of support for schools, performance-based accountability, and extensive public engagement.[3] It is likely that cities adopting constitutional governance will have to organize their transitions in similar ways.

Based on annual progress ratings done by the Portfolio District Network,[4] it is clear that while many cities are progressing rapidly, most are a very long way from fully implementing any of the components. New York City, for example, which has adopted pupil-based finding for schools, still keeps a large share of all funds out of the student backpack in order to pay for a large central office bureaucracy. Baltimore, which has adopted the principle of school autonomy, still requires all schools to abide by the district-wide collective bargaining agreement and taxes all schools to pay for centrally provided services that are used only by some.

Portfolio districts differ profoundly on their approach to school autonomy, with some regarding autonomy as a first step toward improvement for all schools and others granting autonomy only as a reward for high performance. In the latter case, cities' progress toward full implementation of the portfolio strategy is fated to be very slow. Legislation to set up the constitutional governance system would lead to greatly accelerated progress.

Although the portfolio strategy cities are a long way from implementing the constitutional governance system outlined in this book, they are making progress toward it. In cities that have not yet adopted the portfolio strategy, these practical changes would require a more abrupt change of direction and lead to a more difficult transition. However, as the portfolio cities have shown, a change in governance does lead to changes in operating principles and the development of new capacities.

This is not to say that the practical changes needed for constitutional governance of K–12 public education will be easy to accomplish. To the contrary, they will be wrenching and conflict laden. As public officials lose their power to pull strings, reallocate funds, and selectively enforce the rules to benefit certain schools, neighborhoods, or students, some of the most organized and influential members of the community will lose their voice and ability to differentially impact education governance. While it is easy to dismiss such losses as pure political patronage or symbolic politics, they matter a great deal to some people. In many school systems, the political purposes of schools have long been their most important ones.

Arguably, there is no one right answer to the question of on whose behalf public schools should be organized. As communities wrestle with these questions, they must recognize that protecting one set of values—as encompassed in the political purpose of public school systems—is often in direct conflict with protecting another set of values—the degree to which those systems fulfill their obligations to teach children effectively. This book has developed a system that does not deny or wish away the reality of politics; instead it channels politics and prevents its spread into areas that require educational problem solving.

This book began with an old question, Can a different kind of governance lead to better outcomes in public education? The governance system developed here provides a new answer.

Notes

PREFACE

1. Paul T. Hill and Josephine Bonan, *Decentralization and Accountability in Public Education* (Santa Monica, CA: RAND, 1991).

2. See Paul T. Hill, "Urban Education," in *Urban America, Policy Choices for America and the Nation*, ed. James Steinberg, David W. Lyon, and Mary Vaiana (Los Angeles: RAND, 1992), 127–52. The ideas presented in 1992 grew into a book published in 1997: Paul T. Hill, Lawrence Pierce, and James Guthrie, *Reinventing Public Education: How Contracting Can Transform America's Schools* (Chicago: University of Chicago Press, 1997).

3. Bruce A. Bimber, *The Decentralization Mirage* (Santa Monica: RAND, 1994). See also Bruce A. Bimber, *School Decentralization: Lessons from the Study of Bureaucracy* (Santa Monica: RAND, 1993).

4. See Paul T. Hill, *School Boards: Focus on School Performance, Not Money and Patronage* (Washington, DC: Progressive Policy Institute, 2003), A much fuller explanation of the strategy and its implementation successes and pitfalls is in Paul T. Hill, Christine Campbell, and Betheny Gross, *Strife and Progress: Portfolio Strategies for Managing Urban Schools* (Washington, DC: Brookings, 2012). For an independent perspective on portfolio management see Katrina E. Bulkley, "Introduction—Portfolio Management Models in Urban School Reform," in *Between Public and Private: Politics, Governance and the New Portfolio Models for Urban School Reform*, ed. Kartina E. Bulkley, Jeffrey M. Henig, and Henry M. Levin (Cambridge: Harvard Education Press, 2010).

5. Hill, Campbell, and Gross, *Strife and Progress.*

6. *Strife and Progress* acknowledges the ways a portfolio strategy can generate conflict and upset those who traditionally benefit most from traditional public education governance. We also suggest how city leaders can manage those conflicts and avoid letting them harm schools. Jeffrey Henig, Katrina Bulkley, and Henry Levin have also identified potential pitfalls and suggested ways they can be avoided by thoughtful design and implementation. Three chapters in their book *Between Public and Private* are particularly relevant: Jeffrey Henig, "Portfolio Management and the Political Economy of Contracting Regimes," 27–54; Jeffrey Henig and Katrina Bulkley, "Where Public Meets Private, Looking Forward," 323–40; and Henry Levin, "A Framework for Designing Governance in Choice and Portfolio Districts," 217–50. In a less measured critique of the portfolio strategy, Kenneth J. Saltman asserts that the conflicts it sparked have caused a "melee" and a student death in Chicago. See Kenneth J. Saltman, "Urban School Decentralization and the Growth of Portfolio Districts" (East Lansing: Great Lakes Center for Education Research and Practice 2010), 12–13.

CHAPTER 1

1. See the fictitious *Not the New York Times*, published by Christopher Cerf and other Journalists during the 1978 newspaper strike.

2. For an excellent review of K–12 governance issues, see Patrick McGuinn and Paul Manna, "Education Governance in America, Who Leads When Everyone Is in Charge?," *Education Governance for the Twenty-First Century, Overcoming the Structural Barriers to School Reform*, ed. Paul Manna and Patrick McGuinn (Washington, DC: Brookings Institution Press, 2013), 1–20. See also Jeffrey Henig and Katrina E. Bulkley, "Where Public Meets Private, Looking Forward," in *Between Public and Private: Politics, Governance and the New Portfolio Models for Urban School Reform*, ed. Kartina E. Bulkley, Jeffrey M. Henig, and Henry M. Levin (Cambridge, MA: Harvard Education Press, 2010), 323–40.

3. McGuinn and Manna, *Education Governance in America*, provides a similar definition of governance: "the process by which formal institutions and actors wield power and make decisions that influence the conditions under which people live in a society." Dominic Brewer and Joanna Smith offer a definition for public education: "Broadly

interpreted, 'governance' includes the institutions that are part of the educational decision making and delivery system, as well as the constituencies that interact with these institutions, and the ways the parts of the system interact with each other. Policies, laws, regulations and informal practices are part of this framework, and are reflected, one way or another, in the behaviors of all those who are involved." See Dominic Brewer and Joanna Smith, *Evaluating the "Crazy Quilt": Educational Governance in California* (Los Angeles: Center on Educational Governance, 2006), 1.

4. Note that this definition does not include schools' internal governance arrangements—whether they are controlled internally by a teacher collaborative, a principal operating as a sole proprietor, a board of directors, or some other arrangement. As subsequent sections will show, there is no reason to believe that external governance should require that every publicly funded school have the same kind of internal governance.

5. See Terry M. Moe and Paul T. Hill, "Governments, Markets, and the Mixed Model of American Education Reform," *Education Week*, April 20, 2011, p. 30.

6. As the senior author has shown elsewhere, conflict in K–12 education is rooted in the facts that children cannot fully understand or advocate for their own long-term interest in education but that all the adult groups associated with schools also see children's interests through lenses colored by their own self-interest. This is why there are so many conflicts among groups that all think they have children's interests at heart. See Paul T. Hill, Christine Campbell, and Betheny Gross, *Strife and Progress: Portfolio Strategies for Managing Urban Schools* (Washington, DC: Brookings Institution Press, 2012).

7. See James B. Guthrie, "School Finance: A History of Expansion," *The Future of Children, Financing Schools* 7, no. 3 (Winter 1997): 24–38. See also Benjamin Scafidi, *The School Staffing Surge: Decades of Employment Growth in America's Public Schools* (Indianapolis: Friedman Foundation, 2012). (The latter report has been criticized for its policy recommendations but not for the facts it provides. See Joydeep Roy, "Review of the School Staffing Surge Part 2," http://nepc.colorado.edu/thinktank/review-school-staffing-surge-2 downloaded March 29, 2013.)

8. Downloaded from http://www.youtube.com/watch?v=9MGYo CNU5es&list=PLF8B22384B6DCD2BE on February 23, 2014.

9. Michael W. Kirst and Frederick M. Wirt, *Political Dynamics of American Education* (Richmond, CA: McCutchan Publishing, 2009).

10. Marjorie Murphy, *Blackboard Unions: The AFT and the NEA, 1900–1980* (Ithaca, NY: Cornell University Press, 1990).

11. Murphy, *Blackboard Unions.*

12. Charles Kerchner, *A Union of Professionals: Labor Relations and Educational Reform* (New York: Teachers College Press, 1993).

13. Murphy, *Blackboard Unions.* See also David K. Cohen and Susan L. Moffit, *The Ordeal of Equality: Did Federal Regulation Fix the Schools?* (Cambridge, MA: Harvard University Press, 2009).

14. For histories of the growth of the federal regulatory role in K–12 education, see Cohen and Moffit, *The Ordeal of Equality,* and Paul T. Hill, "Schools, Bureaucracy, and the Federal Role in Education," in *Brookings Papers on Education Policy 2000,* ed. Diana Ravitch (Washington, DC: Brookings Institution Press, 2000).

15. Martin West and Paul Peterson, eds., *School Money Trials: The Legal Pursuit of Educational Adequacy* (Washington, DC: Brookings Institution Press, 2006). See also Thomas Timar, "The Institutional Role of State Education Departments: A Historical Perspective," *American Journal of Education,* 105, no. 3 (1997): 231–60.

16. Kenneth K. Wong, et al., *The Education Mayor: Improving America's Schools* (Washington, DC: Georgetown University Press, 2007).

17. See, for example, Nelson Smith, *The Louisiana Recovery School District: Lessons for the Buckeye State* (Washington, DC: Thomas B. Fordham Institute, 2012). See also Robin Baker, Kelly Hupfeld, and Pasul Teske, *Turnarounds in Colorado: Partnering for Innovative Reform in a Local Control State* (Denver: Buchner Institute of Government, University of Colorado Denver, 2013).

18. Terry M. Moe, "The Politics of Bureaucratic Structure," in *Can the Government Govern,* ed. John E. Chubb and Paul E. Peterson (Washington, DC: Brookings Institution Press, 1989), 267–329.

19. Charles T. Kerchner, David Menefee-Libey, and Laura Mulfinger, *Learning from LA: Institutional Change in American Public Education* (Cambridge, MA: Harvard Education Press, 2008).

20. Jeffrey Henig, *The End of Exceptionalism in American Education: The Changing Politics of School Reform* (Cambridge, MA: Harvard Education Press, 2012).

21. For extensive critiques of existing governance arrangements, see Noel Epstein, *Who's in Charge Here: The Tangled Web of School Gover-*

nance and Policy (Washington, DC: Brookings Institution Press, 2004). See also Brewer and Smith, *Evaluating the "Crazy Quilt."*

22. ACT, *STEM Educator Pipeline: Doing the Math on Recruiting Math and Science Teachers* (Iowa City, IA: ACT, 2013).

23. U.S. Department of Education, *Comparability of State and Local Expenditures among Schools within Districts: A Report from the Study of School-Level Expenditures* (Washington, DC: U.S. Department of Education, 2011). See also Ary Spatig-Amerikaner, *Unequal Education: Federal Loophole Enables Lower Spending on Students of Color* (Washington, DC: Center for American Progress, 2012).

24. See Donald Boyd, Hamilton Lankford, Susanna Loeb, and James Wykoff, "Teacher Layoffs: An Empirical Illustration of Seniority versus Measures of Effectiveness," *Journal of Education Finance and Policy* 6, no. 3 (2001): 439–54.

25. Charles Clotfelter, Helen F. Ladd, Jacob Vigdor, and Justin Wheeler, *High Poverty Schools and the Distribution of Teachers and Principals* (Washington, DC: National Center for Analysis of Longitudinal Data in Education Research, 2006).

26. Clarence N. Stone et al., *Building Civic Capacity: The Politics of Reforming Urban Schools* (Lawrence, KS: University Press of Kansas, 2001).

27. Anthony S. Bryk, Penny Bender Sebring, David Kerbow, Sharon Rollow, and John Q. Easton, *Charting Chicago School Reform: Democratic Localism as a Lever for Change* (Boulder, CO: Westview Press, 1998).

28. For a more complete account on the constraints imposed on the use of evidence to determine uses of public funds, see Paul T. Hill, Marguerite Roza, and James Harvey, *Facing the Future: Financing Productive Schools* (Seattle: Center on Reinventing Public Education, 2008).

29. Brewer and Smith, *Evaluating the "Crazy Quilt."*

30. Political scientists suggest that such institutional layering stems from a mismatch between an institution's intensions and its actual outcomes. See Kathleen Thelen, "How Institutions Evolve: Insights from Comparative-Historical Analysis," in *Comparative Historical Analysis in the Social Sciences*, ed. J. Mahoney and D. Rusechemeyer (New York: Cambridge University Press, 2003), 208–40.

31. See the UMass Donahue Institute Research and Evaluation Group, "Superintendent Satisfaction Survey: Summary of Findings" (Boston, MA: Massachusetts Department of Elementary and Secondary Education, 2012).

32. Michael W. Kirst and Frederick M. Wirt, *The Political Dynamics of American Education* (Richmond, CA: McCutchan Publishing Corporation, 2009).

33. John Chubb and Terry M. Moe, *Politics, Markets, and America's Schools* (Washington, DC: Brookings Institution Press, 1990).

34. Wong et al., *The Education Mayor*. See also Kenneth Wong and Francis Shen, *City and State Takeover as a School Reform Strategy*, http://www.ericdigests.org/2003-2/city.html downloaded November 7, 2011.

35. Chester E. Finn Jr., "Reinventing Local Control," *Education Week*, January 23, 1991, p. 40.

36. Jennifer A. O'Day and Marshall S. Smith, "Systemic Reform and Educational Opportunity," in *Designing Coherent Education Policy: Improving The System*, ed. Susan H. Fuhrman (San Francisco, CA: Jossey-Bass, 1993), 250–312.

37. See, for example, "ABC News: Teachers' Union Endorses Obama Despite Hating His Policies," http://abcnews.go.com/Politics/obama-passes-teacherstestbarely/story?id=14003658#.TrxmOuvR1mA, accessed November 10, 2011.

CHAPTER 2

1. See Deborah Stone, *Policy Paradox: The Art of Political Decision Making*, 3d ed. (New York: W. W. Norton Company, 2012).

2. Henry Levin proposes a set of criteria for educational choice systems that overlaps with ours, including freedom to choose, productive efficiency, equity, and social cohesion. See Henry Levin, "A Framework for Designing Governance and Choice in Portfolio Districts," *Between Public and Private*, 217–50.

3. For example, class size mandates are probably neither the surest nor the least expensive way to increase system-wide performance but remain popular nonetheless.

4. Henry Levin's fourth criterion for the design of choice systems, social cohesion, overlaps with our equal opportunity criterion in that equal opportunity is the best possible means of ensuring social cohesion. Levin is also concerned that schools of choice not be allowed to teach divisive ideologies or create distinct cohorts of children who have incompatible values. He would not, however, propose standardization of curriculum or teaching methods. We think his concerns about social cohesion are best met by our two criteria of equitable distribution of op-

portunity and democratic control. For more on the links between equal opportunity and social cohesion see National Working Commission on Choice in K–12 Education, *School Choice: Doing It the Right Way Makes a Difference* (Washington, DC: Brookings Institution Press, 2003).

5. For an up-to-date collection of evidence about system inequities, see "About the Crisis," The Alliance for Excellent Education at http://www.all4ed.org/about_the_crisis, accessed July 25, 2013.

6. "About the Crisis."

7. "About the Crisis."

8. Robert Balfanz, John M. Bridgeland, Mary Bruce, and Joanna Hornig Fox, *Building a Grad Nation: Progress and Challenge in Ending the High School Dropout Epidemic* (Washington, DC: Civic Enterprises, 2013).

9. National Center for Education Statistics, *The Nation's Report Card* (Washington, DC: NCES, 2013).

10. See chapters 3–6 and 10 in Jane Hannaway and Andrew J. Rotherham, *Collective Bargaining in Education: Negotiating Change in Today's Schools* (Cambridge, MA: Harvard Education Press, 2006).

11. Marguerite Roza, *Allocation Anatomy: How District Policies That Deploy Resources Can Support (or Undermine) District Reform Strategies*, School Finance Redesign Project Working Paper 24 (Seattle: Center on Reinventing Public Education, University of Washington, 2007).

12. See U.S. Department of Education, Comparability of State and Local Expenditures; Ary Spatig-Amerikaner, Unequal Education; Marguerite Roza, "How the Current Governance of Education Inhibits Better Uses of Resources," in *Education Governance for the Twenty-First Century*, ed. Patrick McGuinn and Paul Manna (Washington, DC: Brookings Institution Press, 2013).

13. On the consequences of nontransparency on the legitimacy of government activities see Suzanne Mettler, *The Submerged State: How Invisible Government Policies Undermine American Democracy* (Chicago: University of Chicago Press, 2011).

14. Marguerite Roza and Paul T. Hill, "How Within-District Spending Inequities Help Some Schools to Fail," in *Brookings Papers on Education Policy 2004*, ed. Diane Ravitch (Washington, DC: Brookings Institution Press, 2004), 201–18.

15. See, for example, Michael Johnaek, "Private Citizenship and School Choice," *Education Policy* 6, no. 2 (June 1992): 139–58.

CHAPTER 3

1. Here we use the terms "constitution" and "constitutional" as James S. Coleman does in his *Foundations of Social Theory*: for any group or social system a constitution is the combination of norms and rules, both written and unwritten, that impose constraints and demands on its members. See James S. Coleman, *Foundations of Social Theory* (Cambridge, MA: Harvard University Press, 1990), 326–7.

2. See Marc Tucker, *Governing American Education: Why This Dry Subject May Hold the Key Advances in American Education* (Washington, DC: Center for American Progress, 2013).

3. For more on this point, see Paul T. Hill, "Picturing a Different Governance Structure," *Rethinking Education Governance for the New Century*, ed. Patrick McGuinn and Paul Manna (Washington, DC: Brookings Institution Press, 2013).

4. On the costs of traditional governance arrangements, see Lydia C. Segal, *Battling Corruption in America's Public Schools* (Boston: Northeastern University Press, 2003).

5. For a particularly poignant example of what happens when employment relationships are not by mutual agreement, see Steven Brill, "The Rubber Room: The Battle over New York City's Worst Teachers," *New Yorker*, August 31, 2009.

6. On the idea of student "backpack" funding, see Marguerite Roza, *Educational Economics: Where Do School Funds Go?* (Washington, DC: Urban Institute, 2010).

7. Roza, *Allocation Anatomy*.

8. See Frederick M. Hess, *School Boards at the Dawn of the 21st Century: Conditions and Challenges of District Governance* (Washington, DC: National School Boards Association, 2002).

9. Ashley Jochim and Paul T. Hill, *Mayoral Intervention: Right for Seattle Schools?* (Seattle: Center on Reinventing Public Education, 2008).

10. See, for example, Meredith Honig, Michael A. Copland, Lydia Rainey, Juli Anna Lorton, and Morena Newton, *School District Central Office Transformation for Teaching and Learning Improvement* (Seattle: Center for the Study of Teaching and Policy, University of Washington, 2010).

11. Michael DeArmond et al. *The Future of School Facilities: Getting ahead of the Curve* (Seattle: Center on Reinventing Public Education, 2002). See also Nelson Smith, "Whose School Buildings Are They

Anyway," *Education Next.* http://educationnext.org/whose-school
-buildings-are-they-anyway/. Accessed July 17, 2013.

12. Anthony S. Bryk, Penny Bender Sebring, Elaine Allensworth,
Stuart Lupescu, and John Q. Easton, *Organizing Schools for Improvement: Lessons from Chicago* (Chicago: University of Chicago Press, 2010),
217–22.

13. As Bryk and colleagues state it, "The real failure [of traditional
governance] lies in not recognizing that . . . differentiated outcomes are
likely to occur, and in not developing appropriate mechanisms to identify these failures and intervene when and where they occur, and in not
developing the organizational capacity to learn from these problems so
that systems gradually become more effective in managing their own
performance improvement. Bryk et al., *Organizing Schools,* 221.

14. See, for example, Eva Gold, Jeffrey Henig, and Elaine Simon,
"Calling the Shots in Public Education: Parents, Politicians, and Educators Clash," *Dissent, A Quarterly of Politics and Culture,* Fall 2011,
downloaded from http://www.dissentmagazine.org/author/evagold on
February 23, 2014.

15. Terry M. Moe, *Teacher Unions and America's Public Schools* (Washington, DC: Brookings Institution Press, 2011), ch. 4.

16. Ted Kolderie, *Creating the Capacity for Change: How and Why
Governors and Legislatures Are Opening a New-Schools Sector in Public
Education* (Washington, DC: Education Week Press, 2007).

17. See Jeffrey R. Henig, Katrina E. Bulkley, and Henry M. Levin,
"Can Portfolio Management Save Urban Schools?" *Education Week,* October 5, 2010. http://www.edweek.org/ew/articles/2010/10/06/06henig
.h30.html, accessed July 17, 2013.

18. See Moe, *Teacher Unions,* ch. 4.

19. States might be slow to include remote rural school districts that
have only a handful of schools and little capacity to attract new talent.
This is not say that rural areas could not benefit from weighted student
funding of schools, greater school-level autonomy and accountability,
and openness to new ideas, for example, from online instruction providers. Some rural areas could also use the new governance to diversify the pool of talent available to schools, by enabling local musicians,
engineers, scientists, and others to teach courses on a part-time basis
in local schools where shortages of human capital often limit course
offerings.

20. Katrina Bulkley, Jolley Bruce Christman, and Eva Gold, "One

Step Back, Two Steps Forward," in *Between Public and Private*, ed. Katrina Bulkley, Jeffrey Henig, Henry Levin (Cambridge, MA: Harvard Education Press, 2011). See also Gold, Henig, and Simon, "Calling the Shots in Public Education."

21. See Luis Fraga and Ann Frost, "Democratic Institutions, Public Engagement, and Latinos in American Public School," in *Public Engagement for Public Education*, ed. Marion Orr and John Rogers (Palo Alto, CA: Stanford University Press, 2011), 117–38.

CHAPTER 4

1. Colorado's Educational Accountability Act of 2009 (SB-09–163) establishes some of these authorities, but constraints on implementation have prevented the state agency from using it aggressively.

2. Institute on Education Law and Policy, *50-State Report on Accountability, State Intervention and Takeover* (Newark, NJ: Institute on Education Law and Policy, 2002).

3. Ashley Jochim and Patrick Murphy, *The Capacity Challenge: What It Takes for State Education Agencies to Support School Improvement* (Seattle: Center on Reinventing Public Education, 2013).

4. See a more detailed critique in Paul T. Hill, "The Federal Role in Education," in Diane Ravitch, *Brookings Papers on Education Policy 2000*, 11–57.

5. Grover Whitehurst, *Choice and Federalism: Redefining the Federal Role in Education* (Palo Alto, CA: Hoover Institution, Stanford University, 2012). See also Joy Resmovits, "NCLB Bills Proliferate As Lamar Alexander, John Kline Introduce Education Measures," *Huffington Post*, June 6, 2013. http://www.huffingtonpost.com/2013/06/06/nclb-bills -lamar-alexander-john-kline_n_3398221.html. Accessed July 18, 2013.

6. Although some states (e.g., Pennsylvania) are characterized as local-control states and state government often defers to local decision making, this amounts to a traditional political accommodation and does not stem from state constitutions. Even in local-control states, local school boards are state instruments.

7. For a deeper analysis of school boards' status as instruments of the state, see Mitchell Price, "Local Control, Special Education Insurance, and Ownership of Facilities," Memorandum to Paul Hill, July 12, 2012, available from the author.

8. Price, "Local Control."

9. Clarence Stone and colleagues suggest that one of the key challenges to sustaining urban school reform is the lack of particularistic

benefits that serve to buttress political coalitions. As a result, concerned actors engage only episodically, resulting in disruption but not reform. See Stone et al., *Building Civic Capacity: The Politics of Reforming Urban Schools* (Lawrence, KS: University Press of Kansas, 2001).

10. Linda Darling-Hammond, *The Flat World and Education: How America's Commitment to Equity Will Determine Our Future* (New York: Teachers College Press, 2010).

11. These changes require parents to seek and use information, a new experience for some. Studies of low-income parents who get choices for the first time show that they value word-of-mouth information from other parents and are interested in performance data but look for the school where they think their child will do best. That is not always the one with the highest average test scores. Over time, as more parents experience choice and get to know others who face similar options, they are likely to become more confident in exercising choice. Universal choice also opens up questions about how children of negligent parents can still get good schooling opportunities. In some cities where all families have choice, specially trained educators make choices for children whose parent or guardian will not fill out the necessary school selection forms. See Paul Teske, Jody Fitzpatrick, and Gabriel Kaplan, *Opening Doors: How Low-Income Parents Search for the Right School* (Seattle: Center on Reinventing Public Education, 2007).

12. Hill, Campbell, and Gross, *Strife and Progress*.

13. See Charles T. Kerchner and Julia E. Koppich, *A Union of Professionals* (New York: Teachers College Press, 1993). See also Charles T. Kerchner, Julia E. Koppich, and Joseph G. Weeres, *United Mind Workers: Unions and Teaching in the Knowledge Society* (Los Angeles: Jossey Bass, 1997).

14. Jennifer L. Steele et al., *The Transformation of a School System: Principal, Teacher and Parent Perceptions of Charter and Traditional Schools in Post-Katrina New Orleans* (Santa Monica, CA: RAND Corporation, 2011).

15. See Mark Schneider, Paul Teske, Melissa Marschall, Michale Mintrom, and Christine Roch, "Institutional Arrangements and the Creation of Social Capital: The Effects of Public School Choice," *American Political Science Review* 91, no. 1 (1997): 82–93. See also David Fleming, "School Vouchers, Social Capital, and Political Participation: Evidence from the Milwaukee Parental Choice Program," Institute for Education Sciences Research Conference, Washington, DC, June 2009.

CHAPTER 5

1. A good example is San Diego, which moved from school empowerment in the late 1980s to a centrally controlled uniform district-wide instructional method in the mid-1990s. See Frederick Hess, ed., *Urban School Reform: Lessons from San Diego* (Cambridge, MA: Harvard Education Press, 2005). See also Julian Betts et al., *From Blueprint to Reality: San Diego's Education Reforms* (San Francisco: Public Policy Institute of California, 2005).

2. Bruce Bimber, *School Decentralization: Lessons in the Study of Bureaucracy* (Santa Monica, CA: RAND Corporation, 1993)

3. Philip K. Howard, *The Death of Common Sense: How Law Is Suffocating America* (New York: Random House: 1994), 11.

4. Organization for Economic Cooperation and Development, *OECD Report on Regulatory Reform: Synthesis* (Paris: OECD, 1997), 14.

5. See, for example, Government Accountability Office, *Charter Schools: Additional Federal Attention Needed to Help Protect Access for Students with Disabilities* (Washington, DC: GAO, 2012).

6. See, for example, Stephanie Simon, "Special Report: Class Struggle—How Charter Schools Get Students They Want," *Reuters*, February 15, 2013.

7. Julie Mead and Preston Green, *Chartering Equity: Using Charter School Legislation and Policy to Advance Equal Educational Opportunity* (Boulder: National Education Policy Center, 2012).

8. Louisiana's law was struck down as impermissibly transferring funds to nonpublic schools in the case of *Louisiana Federation of Teachers et al. v. State of Louisiana, Supreme Court of Louisiana*, no. 2013-CA-0120, May 7, 2013.

9. Bruno Manno, "The Accountability Puzzle," in Chester E. Finn, Bruno Manno, and Greg Vanourek, *Charter Schools in Action* (Princeton NJ: Princeton University Press, 2000).

10. On the meaning and practical use of this term, see Edwin P. James, Termination for Default and for the Convenience of the Government, *Boston College Law Review*, 5, no. 1 (1963): 65–78.

11. These conclusions are based on the authors' unpublished interviews and focus groups with New York City principals and with English school heads, particularly in Specialist Schools and Academies. No formal studies directly assess this issue, but principals and school heads organizations consistently oppose new requirements that reduce

autonomy. See, for example, Helen Zelon, "New York's School Principals Struggle Quietly amid Teacher Controversies," *City Limits*, Friday, July 29, 2011. http://www.citylimits.org/news/articles/4359/new-york-s-school-principals-struggle-quietly-amid-teacher-contr/#.UfFT gKXvwzY. Accessed July 25, 2013.

CHAPTER 6

1. This leads to an additional function that many superintendents acknowledge: providing employment for tenured educators whom no one wants in the schools. This function helps explain the low regard some school leaders have of central office effectiveness.

2. Roza, *Allocation Anatomy*.

3. David Tyack, *The One Best System: A History of American Urban Education* (Cambridge, MA: Harvard University Press, 1974).

4. As reported by David Arsen and Yongmei Ni, charters spend on average nearly $400 less per pupil than districts on instructional support services like student services, libraries, and curriculum specialists. This is so despite the charters' much smaller scale than districts. See David Arsen and Yongmei Ni, *Is Administration Leaner in Charter Schools? Resource Allocation in Charter and Traditional Public Schools* (New York: National Center for the Study of Privatization in Education, 2012).

5. This was driven by funding formulas that allocated staff using fixed ratios per school as well as by centrally managed collective bargaining agreements that enabled senior staff to concentrate in low poverty schools. See Roza, *Allocation Anatomy*.

6. For an elaboration on the role of headquarters in a divisonalized firm, see Oliver E. Williamson, *Markets and Hierarchies, Analysis and Antitrust Implications: A Study in the Economics of Internal Organization* (New York: Free Press, 1975).

7. See Nicolai J. Foss, "On Rationales of Corporate Headquarters," *Industrial and Corporate Change* 6, no. 2 (1997): 313–38.

8. David Osborne and Ted Gaebler, *Reinventing Government: How the Entrepreneurial Spirit Is Transforming the Public Sector* (Reading, MA: Addison-Wesley, 1992).

9. See Helen F. Ladd, "Education Inspectorate Systems in New Zealand and the Netherlands," *Education Finance and Policy* 5, no. 3 (2010): 378–92.

10. See Malcolm K. Sparrow, *The Regulatory Craft: Controlling Risk,*

Solving Problems and Managing Compliance (Washington, DC: Brookings Institution Press, 2000).

CHAPTER 7

1. The ideas in this section are developed at greater length in two recent papers: Paul T. Hill, "School Finance in the Digital Learning Era," in *Education Reform for the Digital Era*, ed. Chester E. Finn and Daniela R. Fairchild (Washington, DC: Thomas B. Fordham Institute 2012); and Paul T. Hill, "Governing Schools for Productivity," *The Productivity for Results Series* (Dallas, TX: George W. Bush Institute's Education Reform Initiative).

2. The Hoover Institution's Koret Task Force has recommended a transformation of the federal role in education that is consistent with this proposal. See Grover Whitehurst, *Choice and Federalism: Defining the Federal Role in Education* (Palo Alto, CA: Hoover Press, 2012).

3. Hill, "School Finance in the Digital Learning Era."

4. For an explanation of the cafeteria plan idea, in this case applied to teacher benefits, see Noah Wepman, Marguerite Roza, and Christina Sepe, *The Promise of Cafeteria-Style Benefits for Districts and Teachers* (Seattle: Center on Reinventing Public Education, 2010).

5. Should parents be allowed to supplement the amounts allowed by the school with their own funds? Supplementation would allow experimentation with a wider range of services, but it would also allow some vendors to serve only the more affluent parents. It is, however, difficult to see how parents could be prevented from buying supplements with their own money.

6. For an explanation of the "adequacy" rationale now in use in school finance litigation, see Eric Hanushek and Alfred A. Lindseth, *Schoolhouses, Courthouses, and Statehouses: Solving the Funding-Achievement Puzzle in America's Public Schools* (Princeton, NJ: Princeton University Press, 2009).

CHAPTER 8

1. Terry M. Moe, *Special Interest: Unions and America's Public Schools* (Washington, DC: Brookings Institution Press, 2011).

2. Of course, executives are not always so well positioned. See Ashley Jochim and Paul Hill, *Mayoral Control: Right for Seattle Schools?* (Seattle: Center on Reinventing Public Education, 2008).

3. See the Ohio General Assembly's June 2012 action (H.B. 525),

changing state law to enable the implementation of the Cleveland Plan, allowing dramatically increased autonomy and flexibility for the district and its schools, the modernization of employment practices, and increased incentives for district and charter school partnerships.

4. See Patrick Murphy and Lydia Rainey, *Modernizing the State Education Agency: Different Paths toward Performance Management* (Seattle: Center on Reinventing Public Education, 2012).

5. Jeffrey Henig, *The End of Exceptionalism in American Education: The Changing Politics of School Reform* (Cambridge, MA: Harvard Education Press, 2013).

6. Hill, Campbell, and Gross, *Strife and Progress*.

7. Jeffrey Henig and Katrina Bulkley offer similar cautions about the portfolio strategy. They identify three risks: that the strategy will be adopted in places that lack the human, financial, and governmental resources required to create quality new educational options; that it will be set in place and then neglected by city leaders, rather than thoughtfully implemented and constantly adjusted in light of experience; and that governmental actors (e.g., the CEC) will not play their roles aggressively enough to counter abuses based on the private interests of school providers, leading to public sector brain drain, hiding of key information based on proprietary rights, underfunding of governmental oversight and research and development, and artificial barriers of entry against new providers. See Jeffrey Henig and Katrina E. Bulkley, *Between Public and Private*, 323–40.

8. As Eric Patashnik notes,

There are three major reasons to expect policy reform victories to prove fleeting. First, and most importantly, the diffuse groups that receive benefits from general-interest reforms will generally face far more difficult burdens of collective action than will those who would profit from the reforms' unraveling ... A second reason why prior reforms can be expected to crumble over time is that the focus of policy-makers, the media, and the general public will predictably shift to other matters ... A final reason why broad-based reforms can be expected to unravel ... [is that they] may be completely bewildering to ordinary voters. As a result of these complexities, citizens may fail to recognize that they have a stake in policy-reform debates. See pp. 209–10 in Eric Patashnik, "After the Public Interest Prevails: The Political Sustainability of Policy Reform," *Governance:*

An International Journal of Policy, Administration, and Institutions 16, no. 2 (April 2003): 203–34.

9. See Christopher R. Berry and William G. Howell, "Accountability and Local Elections: Rethinking Retrospective Voting," *Journal of Politics* 69, no. 3 (2007): 844–58.

10. See Paul T. Hill, Christine Campbell, and James Harvey, *It Takes a City: Getting Serious about Urban School Reform* (Washington, DC: Brookings, 2000).

11. Kenneth Saltman, p. 13, tells of a bungled high school closing in Chicago that forced students to enroll in schools that they could reach only by crossing gang lines. This tragic story illustrates the consequences of lax implementation of the portfolio strategy. See Kenneth J. Saltman, *Urban School Decentralization and the Growth of Portfolio Districts* (East Lansing, MI: Great Lakes Center for Education Research and Practice 2010), 12–13.

12. John Engberg, Brian Gill, Gema Zamarro, and Ron Zimmer, "Closing Schools in a Shrinking District: Do Student Outcomes Depend on Which Schools Are Closed?" *Journal of Urban Economics* 71, no. 2 (2012): 189–203.

13. See, for example the story about seventeen Columbus, Ohio, charter schools closing in one year. http://www.dispatch.com//content/stories/local/2014/01/12/charter-failure.html. Downloaded February 25, 2014.

14. Paul T. Hill and Kacey Guin, "Baselines for Assessment of Choice Programs," *Education Policy Analysis Archives* 11, no. 39 (October 2003).

CHAPTER 9

1. Hill, Campbell, and Gross, *Strife and Progress*.

2. New Orleans, New York City, Chicago, Denver, Cleveland, Baltimore, Hartford, New Haven, Boston, Rhode Island Mayors' Academy, Detroit, Minneapolis, Milwaukee, Memphis, Columbus, Indianapolis, Cincinnati, Nashville, Jefferson Parish LA, Spring Branch TX, Austin, Oakland, Sacramento, Spokane, Washington, DC.

3. For a full explanation of portfolio strategy components, see http://www.crpe.org/portfolio/components.

4. For up-to-date ratings and explanations, see http://www.crpe.org/portfolio/components.

Index

Page numbers followed by the letter *t* indicate tables.